TRADING BINARY OPTIONS

The Bloomberg Financial Series provides both core reference knowledge and actionable information for financial professionals. The books are written by experts familiar with the work flows, challenges, and demands of investment professionals who trade the markets, manage money, and analyze investments in their capacity of growing and protecting wealth, hedging risk, and generating revenue.

Since 1996, Bloomberg Press has published books for financial professionals on investing, economics, and policy affecting investors. Titles are written by leading practitioners and authorities, and have been translated into more than 20 languages.

For a list of available titles, please visit our website at www.wiley.com/go/bloombergpress.

TRADING BINARY OPTIONS

Strategies and Tactics

Second Edition

Abe Cofnas

WILEY

Cover image: © styleTTT/istockphoto
Cover design: Wiley

Copyright © 2016 by Abe Cofnas. All rights reserved.

Published by John Wiley & Sons, Inc., Hoboken, New Jersey.

The first edition was published by John Wiley & Sons, Inc. in November 2011.

Published simultaneously in Canada.

For general information on our other products and services or for technical support, please contact our
Customer Care Department within the United States at (800) 762-2974, outside the United States at
(317) 572-3993, or fax (317) 572-4002.

Wiley publishes in a variety of print and electronic formats and by print-on-demand. Some material
included with standard print versions of this book may not be included in e-books or in print-on-
demand. If this book refers to media such as a CD or DVD that is not included in the version you
purchased, you may download this material at http://booksupport.wiley.com. For more information
about Wiley products, visit www.wiley.com.

Library of Congress Cataloging-in-Publication Data:

Names: Cofnas, Abe, 1950- author.
Title: Trading binary options : strategies and tactics / Abe Cofnas.
Description: Second edition. | Hoboken, New Jersey : John Wiley & Sons, 2016.
 | Includes index.
Identifiers: LCCN 2016014537| ISBN 978-1-119-19417-0 (cloth) |
 ISBN 978-1-119-19419-4 (epub) | ISBN 978-1-119-19418-7 (ePDF)
Subjects: LCSH: Options (Finance) | Prices—Forecasting.
Classification: LCC HG6024.A3 C635 2016 | DDC 332.64/53—dc23
LC record available at https://lccn.loc.gov/2016014537

FSC
www.fsc.org
MIX
Paper from
responsible sources
FSC® C101537

Printed in the United States of America.
10 9 8 7 6 5 4 3 2 1

Contents

Preface

Are you interested in trading, but don't like to wait weeks and months for a return? Are you following news events and want to financially benefit from your knowledge? Are you new to trading and want to participate but avoid the long learning curve for mastering trading skills? If these questions are on your mind, this book is for you.

Binary option trading provides excitement and opportunity for achieving unusually large returns in less than a week! While there are many variations to this type of trading, this book focuses on the regulatory-approved weekly binary option trades of the North American Derivative Exchange (Nadex). Trades have limited risk to the cost of a position. There is no margin. The trade is a bet on the direction of a market by the end of the week. If the trade is correct, the payoff is $100 per lot. If it is wrong, the payoff is $0. Simply put, it's a yes-or-no proposition. One can open an account with as little as $100 and start trading. This simple structure allows anyone to trade in over 20 different underlying markets, from currencies to indexes to commodities.

This book takes the reader through the basic features of the binary option instrument. But it does more. It provides a detailed review of fundamental and technical analysis useful to making trading decisions. Beginners, as well as more experienced traders, will be able to build upon their core trading knowledge. More importantly, new online tools and techniques for detecting market sentiment are presented, because trading can no longer be separated from the Internet and the social media it has generated. The web itself is a force on trading decisions and outcomes, as emotions are propagated through the web. This phenomenon has made sentiment analysis a major challenge for traders. For the binary option trader who is shaping a decision for a weekly outcome, or even an intraday outcome, the critical factor will be the actionable knowledge that is applied.

This book provides real-world examples of how to scan the political and economic news and formulate appropriate binary option trading strategies. Key trading strategies are reviewed with examples. These include: *at-the-money; out-of-the-money; in-the-money; deep-in-the-money;* and *deep-out-of-the-money*. Also reviewed are case studies of binary option trading in relationship to key news events that we have lived through. These include: The U.S. congressional elections; the Greek sovereign risk crises; turmoil in the Middle East; and the Japanese earthquake. The reader will see exactly how these events shaped trading strategies that worked.

This book is also designed to provide a self-directed performance audit capability to the trader. Specific training challenges are provided, including a test of your knowledge (see Appendix A).

No other book provides a comprehensive get-started approach to trading binary options. It is my hope that *Trading Binary Options: Strategies and Tactics* makes a difference and improves your ability to get started in binary option trading, but most importantly, to do it the right way!

Acknowledgments

This book would not have been possible without the support of many people. First, I want to thank Agora Financial Inc., and, in particular, Addison Wiggin, for his support in my development of binary options analysis and alerts for the *Binary Dimensions* newsletter. The experience of a weekly provision of real-time alerts and analysis of binary options has provided an invaluable base of knowledge that made this book possible. Joseph Shriefer and Rick Barnard of the Agora Financial team have also provided valuable input on my analyses. The North American Derivative Exchange (Nadex) has been of great assistance in providing access to technical information and data used in this book. None of the opinions or alerts in this book has been subject to any prior review or approval by Agora Financial Inc. or Nadex. Dean Reese, Bryant Lie, Zach Tyvand, and Bill Egan provided important research support. Finally, thanks go to my wife, Paula, who provided the support and goodwill at home that sustained me during the intense writing period.

A.C.

About the Author

Abe Cofnas is considered a leader in the field of currency trading, analysis, and training. He founded learn4x.com (www.learn4x.com) in 2001 as one of the first online training programs for currency trading. He has been the Forex trader columnist for *Modern Trader* magazine since 2001, writing over 100 columns on Forex events.

He has authored three previous books on trading: *The Forex Trading Course: A Self-Study Guide to Becoming a Successful Currency Trader* (now in its second edition); *The Forex Options Course: A Self-Study Guide to Trading Currency Options; and Sentiment Indicators—Renko, Price Break, Kagi, Point and Figure: What They Are and How to Use Them to Trade.* He is also the editor of Binary Dimensions newsletter, which specializes in binary option alerts.

He brings extensive understanding of trading from all perspectives, including advanced fundamental and political analysis. Cofnas holds two master's degrees from the University of California at Berkeley—a master's in political science and a master's in public policy analysis. He is Senior Fundamental Strategist for the Market Trader's Institute.

Cofnas can be reached at abecofnas@gmail.com.

INTRODUCTION

What Are Binary Options and Why Are They Important?

Let's get right to the point and answer the question: What are binary options? *Binary options* are a type of option instrument that provide a fixed deadline for expiration, with a fixed payout. Basically, it is a yes or no bet. Specifically, the bet is on whether a settled price of an underlying market will be at, above, or below a target strike barrier, by a defined future time. For example, on a Monday morning, the trader is trying to answer the question: Will the S&P be at 1350 by Friday at 4 p.m.? If the trader anticipated this outcome, and turned out to be right, the payoff using the North American Derivatives Exchange (Nadex) binary options would be $100 per unit. If another index—the S&P 500, for example—did not reach this level, the payoff would be zero dollars. If the trader is correct, the return can approach extraordinary levels of 500 percent and more for only five days of play. This book will show you how it is possible for the average person to achieve extraordinary profits with binary option trading.

The binary option is called *binary* because it fits the condition of being either right or wrong—all or nothing. Binary option trading fits right into the digital era, which is based on binary logic. In fact, the binary options offered by Nadex can be considered to be part of a type of option classified as European Digital Options. But the question arises: Why are binary options important? There are many reasons that come to mind. Binary options are important, but not simply because they are a relatively new trading

1

instrument. In fact, they are not really new. They have been used for decades at institutional levels as an *over-the-counter* instrument but, most significantly, traders in the United States have used them since 2008 when they became approved by the Commodity Futures Trading Commission (CFTC) and regulated through the Nadex. They are often called *rebate options* because of their use to generate a payment as a form of insurance when damage occurs. But let's get back to the question. Binary options are important because they offer to the trader, in one instrument, the ability to succeed at many levels that go beyond simply obtaining a winning trade.

Binary options are an ideal trading instrument for new traders to test their skills because at a core level, binary option trading starts with anticipating direction. Being right on direction is one of the most important skills relevant to trading any market. In fact, being wrong on direction accounts for a majority of the losses occurred in any trading. Another key skill important for mastering binary option trading is risk management. A binary option trade is not necessarily a set-and-let decision. This kind of strategy is followed when a position is put on and thereafter the trader watches the screen and sees what happens at the end of the week. Set-and-let trading does not involve managing the trade during its duration. Sometimes this is an effective strategy. However, trading binary options requires a sharp sense of timing. It's important for the trader to know when conditions are ripe for entry as well as when market conditions have changed enough to justify getting out of the way. Honing entry and exit skills in binary option trading can be transferred to other markets.

Binary options are also important because they offer a level playing field. Anyone can trade the binaries and at very low costs ranging from $5 to $90 per lot at any moment. Because the time frame is at most one week, binary option trading counters the observed tendency of traders to hold losers too long and sell winners too soon (Odean 1998).

But there are even more reasons that contribute to the value of binary option trading. Binary options offer beginning traders the ability to explore over 20 different markets. In a sense, binary option trading presents a discount tour of global markets. Perhaps one of the most important reasons of all is that binary options are regulated (through the Nadex) and offer price transparency. In this post-Madoff era of scrutiny and skepticism, trading binary options that are regulated becomes more and more salient to traders. That is why this book focuses on the regulated binary options offered at the Nadex exchange. For those who want to trade the binary option instruments that are over the counter, the skills built in trading the Nadex instruments will apply.

Binary options are an exciting product. In fact, traders in the United States have responded by participating at increased volume levels of around 30 to 50 percent per month! At this pace of volume growth, binary trading can one day become as big as forex trading, which is now approaching $5 trillion per day. In an email exchange with John Austin, the CEO of IG Markets Group North America, and a key player in creating the binary option product, he says: "There is really no competing product. I feel quite strongly that for smaller retail traders, the capped-risk nature of binaries is hugely important. Nadex's contracts allow traders to speculate on global financial markets while using only a limited amount of risk capital and without leaving themselves open to catastrophic losses in the event of unexpected market volatility. For this reason, I believe they may become the product of choice for those who are just starting out in trading. In addition, I think their small size and self-contained nature will mean they will become the default choice for more experienced traders looking for a cheap real-money way to test out new technical analysis-based trading systems, as well as being an additional toolkit used by conventional futures and FX traders alongside their more conventional trading."

Let's delve a bit into the psycho-dynamic aspects of binary option trading, because, as you will see later in this book, trading binary options is not only a fundamental and technical analysis endeavor, but it is also concomitantly a psychological behavioral experience. This points to another reason that binary options are exciting: their similarity to gambling. A binary option trade has been often viewed or referred to as a bet. This is metaphorically true, but not in fact correct. Betting in gambling is quite different from a binary option bet. In gambling, the bettors face the same fixed odds and cannot affect the probability of winning. A bet in a gambling activity is indeed a passive ride. Whether it's the roll of the dice, or the drawing of a card in a game of poker, the gambler is riding a *probability wave*. Finally, a gambling bet is associated with a probability about what proportion of time an outcome should occur. A binary option bet is quite different. It cannot be associated with a statistically predictable outcome.

The binary option trade is certainly a ride, but on a *sentiment wave*. It is also not a passive experience, and it is one that demands attention because the odds of winning are not a function of statistics. Instead, and in direct contradiction to the gambling situation, the odds of winning are determined by the skills of the trader in assessing market conditions and managing risk. In a roll of the dice, the next outcome is independent of the previous roll. In contrast, in binary trades, the next trade outcome is linked to the market behavior during the previous outcome! In gambling, the prevailing law is the law of large numbers in which, eventually, winning and losing streaks offset each other. In binary option trading, winning and losing streaks are not statistical outcomes.

Binary option trading is a prime example of the value of actionable knowledge. The binary option trader is participating in an imperfect-information game, where it's never possible to have all the information necessary to win. It clearly takes a certain level of knowledge to play this game well. We will explore what kind of fundamental and technical skills are necessary to develop oneself into a binary option trader in greater detail in later chapters.

Nadex versus CBOT Binaries

In any case, *Nadex binary options* are important because they are the fastest growing segment of exchange-listed binary options. But it is important to point out that the Chicago Board of Trade (CBOT) does offer binary options on *event risks*. These include the CME Hurricane Index, the Snowfall Index, and the Target Fed Funds. However, the *CBOT binary options* remain very small in volume, are highly illiquid, and are really tailored for institutions like insurance companies (see www.cboe.com/products/indexopts/bsz_spec.aspx for a list of CBOE binary options).

There are several differences between the CBOE and the Nadex binaries that should be clarified. First, the CBOE binary options use the cash index as the underlying market for the contract. In contrast, the Nadex binaries (except for currencies as the underlying market) use the futures index. More important, the CBOE binaries have a much wider *bid-offer spread*. Remember that buyers pay the ask price, and sellers pay the bid price. This creates a spread, which generates money to the firm. It is also important to note that the CBOE binaries have a much lower liquidity than Nadex binaries. It also appears that the CBOE volume is constantly very low, in the range of a few hundred contracts per month. In contrast, the Nadex sees volumes in excess of 100,000 lots per month. During the important May 2 week when huge sell-offs occurred in the markets, CBOE's S&P binary option volume was close to zero, while Nadex had a volume of 38,682 lots on all U.S. indexes.

The differences in the duration of the binary options are also important to note. CBOE binary options have expirations of a variety of months: one-month, two-month, and three-month expiration. The Nadex expirations are much shorter in duration. They are intraday, daily, and weekly. This means that by Friday at 4:15 P.M., all binary option contracts expire, giving the trader a fresh, new start every week. These differences point to Nadex as having a significant advantage for traders who want to experience market action. High volume fuels the power of options and is a critical condition for traders—the Nadex fulfills that need. Lastly, Nadex binaries offer a logical place to start. The skills acquired for trading in Nadex can help prepare you for trading options in other markets.

In the near future, however, the popularity of Nadex options will surely spur other imitators. There are many binary option over-the-counter firms worldwide that provide different forms of binary options. These include, but are not limited to *one-touch* and *no-touch options*, as well as *range options*. One-touch options are trades in which a win occurs if the price touches a certain point. In these options, the trader is betting that either a resistance point or a support point will be touched by the price by a certain time. A no-touch option is a bet that the particular price point will not be touched by a certain time. A range option presents the bet that the price will stay in between two strike prices, or go through one of them by a certain time. Some of these innovative binary trades are very short, with expiration time frames of minutes. Also, in some overseas firms, the trader determines the size of the payout! In principle, the skills developed trading the Nadex options can enable effective trading of binary options, and other, perhaps more complex and sophisticated, options. So let's explore the key features of Nadex binary options in greater detail.

Reference

Odean, T. 1998. "Are Investors Reluctant to Realize Their Losses?" *Journal of Finance* 53: 1775–1798.

CHAPTER 1

Key Features of Binary Option Types

This chapter covers the key features of a binary option contract available globally and in the United States. There are two basic types of binary option trades. The first is the laddered binary options offered at the Nadex Exchange, part of the IG Markets, the Cantor Exchange, the CBOE, the CBOT, and the NYSE binaries, also known as Byrds. The NYSE binaries launched in 2016 and offer binaries on equities. The NYSE entry into binaries allows traders to trade weekly binaries on major equities. The CBOE offers binaries on the VIX and announced binaries on the China A50 index. These are potential game changers for traders who look to use binaries as part of their total trading toolbox.

Nadex and the Cantor Exchange are CFTC approved. Nadex is owned by IG Markets. The Cantor Exchange, owned by Cantor Fitzgerald, is a true exchange and does not make a market in the binaries. In other words, they don't take the other side of a trade placed by a customer. Instead, liquidity is supplied by independent market makers. The second type of binary option trades is the non-laddered platform, simply offering the opportunity to bet on the whether the price will be higher or lower at expiration. These are not currently allowed in the United States, but are popular around the world.

Later in the chapter, I also discuss the four basic strategies of trading—at-the-money, in-the-money, out-of-the-money, and deep-in/out-the-money—as well as the role of the market maker in the process. The chapter will end with a sample bid/ask scenario.

Defining the Key Features

Let's start by defining the features that shape most of the laddered binary option selection and trading. These terms will be used time and again throughout this book, so commit these definitions to memory. You'll come to know them well.

Expiration date: The time that the option expires.

Settlement value: The value of the option on expiration. It will be $0 or a $100-fixed payout.

Underlying market price: This is the actual real-time market price of the underlying contract.

Contract: This is the basic unit of a trade of one lot. The value of a lot varies among firms. For example, one lot at Cantor is $1. One lot at Nadex is $100. At IG, 0.01 lots is $100.

Bid: The premium price that a trader receives for opening to sell a contract.

Buy: This refers to betting the underlying market will go up. A trader opens a trade and pays the ask price associated with a strike price. If the price settles above the strike price, then the trader wins the $100 ask price.

Sell: This refers to betting the underlying market will go down. A trader puts on an open sell order. The trader pays for an open sell order ($100 – bid). It is $100 – (bid). This is equal to putting on a position, anticipating a decrease in the price of the underlying market. It is also the premium price that a trade pays for closing a position that was bought. The sell is also labeled as the put tab at the Cantor Exchange

Spread: The difference between the bid and the ask. With any new market, the spread will tend to be narrow as more volume increases.

Bid size/offer size: This is the number of positions being bought or sold. You will find that the bid and offer size is not useful as an indicator of sentiment.

Commission fee: The trader may pay a commission fee per transaction. Nadex charges $1 per transaction. Firms offering Nadex binaries may be offering different commissions.

Start time: At the Nadex, IG markets, and Cantor Exchanges, the start time for a binary trader is fixed at the beginning of an interval. A five-minute trade interval starts, for example, at 05:00 and ends at 05:05. A trader can enter the trade before the expiration, but the time to expiration is not triggered by the entry. In other platforms (discussed later), a rolling start is featured. This means whenever the trader puts on a trade, the trade duration clock starts at that point and ends at the designated duration.

Settlement value: This is the price the binary firm uses to determine whether the trade is a winner or loser. Notice that there is no agreement between different firms on what is the settlement value. There are different formulas among different firms for determining settlement value. Of particular importance is that settlement value of binary option underlying markets among offshore firms (not regulated in United States, London, or Australia) are often manipulated to reduce winners.

Expiration duration: Binary expirations refer to the duration of the option. Among global platforms, durations run the board from one-minute to one-week expirations.

Note: The principles of trading binaries apply to all time frames. The short time frames involve more timing skills, and require a focus on momentum indicators and pattern breaks. Longer time frames, such as one day and more, allow fundamentals to influence the price patterns.

Notice that missing here are the option features known as the Greeks—Delta, Theta, Vega, Volga, and so on. They are not really missing. It's just that they are not necessary to trading weekly or intraday binary options that offer fixed payouts.

Strike Price versus Underlying Market Price

Binary options featuring a laddered approach have several features that need to be thoroughly understood. Some of these features will be familiar to option traders and are common to all options.

The first feature to understand is the *strike price.* This is the price target a trader anticipates the price will hit at expiration time: at the target, above the target, or below the target. It is important to note that there can be up to 14 strike prices listed by the Nadex Exchange for each underlying contract. When you have a set of strike prices to trade, they are called a *ladder.*

For example, at Nadex and IG, the weekly binary option ladders are statements in which the trader decides to buy the binary option if he agrees it will be greater than the associated strike price. If the trader believes the settlement will be lower than the associated strike price, the trade that is put on is a sell. See Table 1.1 for examples of binary option ladders. Notice that the strike price closest to the indicative price (which is the market price of the underlying contract) has an ask value near 50. It is always the case that the market price closest to the ask price will be valued near 50.

TABLE 1.1 Snapshot of Binary Contract and Strike Prices

Contract Strike Price	Expiration	Bid	Offer	Indicative
Gold (Feb16) > 1094.5	18-Dec-15	9.50	17.50	1066.7
Gold (Feb16) > 1084.5	18-Dec-15	19.50	27.75	1066.7
Gold (Feb16) > 1074.5	18-Dec-15	33.25	41.50	1066.7
Gold (Feb16) > 1064.5	18-Dec-15	48.75	57.00	1066.7
Gold (Feb16) > 1054.5	18-Dec-15	64.00	72.25	1066.7
Gold (Feb16) > 1044.5	18-Dec-15	77.00	85.00	1066.7
Gold (Feb16) > 1034.5	18-Dec-15	86.00	94.25	1066.7

Another component to understand is the *underlying market*. The binary option specifically tracks a particular market known as the underlying market. The underlying market for index-related binary strike prices are, except for the currency pairs, the near-term futures contracts. For example, a trader wanting to put on a position on gold would be watching not only the gold spot market, but the gold futures contract that is trading on the Commodity Exchange, Inc. (Comex). Similarly, if a trader wants to trade the S&P 500 binary at Nadex, the actual underlying market is the active future contract. The fact that the underlying markets may be a futures contract on the markets does not pose difficulties. The fact is that the spot and near-term futures contract for these markets move in close tandem to each other. But the exact settlement price is in the futures contract and not the underlying spot market, except for the currencies.

The updated list of what markets can be traded at these exchanges can be easily tracked at their respective websites (Table 1.2).

TABLE 1.2 Binary Platforms

Firm	Website
North American Derivative Exchange (Nadex)	www.nadex.com
IG	www.igmarkets.com
NYSE ByRDs	https://www.nyse.com/products/options-byrds
CBOE	https://www.cboe.com/micro/binaries/introduction.aspx
Cantor Exchange	www.cantorexchange.com

Currency Pairs as an Underlying Market

At Nadex IG and the Cantor Exchange, binary options are available on the majors and many cross pairs. USD/JPY, USD/CAD, USD/CHF, EUR/USD, GBP/USD, EUR/JPY, GBP/JPY, AUD/JPY, and the AUD/USD. This is a broad enough range of currency pairs to enable the trader to play almost any strategy and correlate that strategy with global market events. The underlying market to track for trading weekly binary currency options is the spot currency market (see Tables 1.2 and 1.3).

Beginning binary traders should consider the weekly expirations. Trading goes from Monday morning at approximately 3 A.M. EST to 3 P.M. EST on Friday. The weekly expirations give the trader time to be right, and time for fundamentals to work on markets. In recent years, Nadex and IG have added 20-minute and 5-minute expirations to their binary option platforms. All the features of the longer daily and weekly durations are present in the short expiration binaries.

Moneyness

One of the most salient relationships to thoroughly understand is where the binary strike price is in relationship to the underlying market. This feature is known in the field of option trading as *moneyness*. Understanding moneyness of the binary option contract generates the ability to gauge market sentiment and, along with it, the expected probability of success of a particular binary option. There are three key metrics to evaluate.

- *At-the-money (ATM):* When the strike price is equal to the underlying market price (the spot). For non-laddered binaries, putting a high-low trade on is in effect an at-the-money trade!
- *In-the-money (ITM):* When the underlying market is greater than the strike price. This occurs when a trader is buying the position. When the trader is opening a position to sell, the option is in-the-money when the underlying market is less than the strike price.
- *Out-of-the-money (OTM):* This occurs when a trader is opening the position to buy and when the underlying market is less than the strike price and the strike price is above the spot market price. This also occurs when a trader is opening a position to sell and the underlying market is greater than the strike price.

We can add two more important variations of the binary option strike price condition: *deep-out-of-the-money* and *deep-in-the-money*. These refer to the outer strike prices or ladders. A good way to think about where they are located from a price point of view is to define deepness in regard to the spot price as a 10 percent probability for out-of-the-money and a 90 percent probability for in-the-money. Few traders would argue that those levels are not deep.

The condition of being *near-the-money* is also a credible way of characterizing the relationship between the binary option strike price and its moneyness.

When the binary strike price is roughly at-the-money, the cost of buying that strike price will be close to $50 per unit because the market interprets an ATM strike price as having an equal probability of going up or down. This means that a scan of actual binary strike price ask prices that are near $50 can, in fact, serve as quick guide to where the underlying spot market is at, without even looking at a chart. It's a good idea to routinely check ATM prices and see the relationship it has with the underlying market.

Moneyness and Trader Direction

When a binary option strike price is in-the-money (ITM), its meaning, as to its profitability, depends on whether the trader has gone long or short. For example, if the trader is putting on a long position, he is expecting the underlying spot market to go up (Table 1.3). In-the-money means that the spot underlying market has already moved above the binary option strike price—the underlying market is greater than the strike price. This is exactly what the trader wants to see happen for profits to be realized. The effect is that the market begins to price higher the cost of buying that contract. The crowd becomes optimistic for the price to remain above the binary strike price.

TABLE 1.3 Moneyness and the Spot Price When Buying Binaries

Moneyness	Relationship to Spot
In-the-money	Underlying market < strike price
At-the-money	Underlying market = strike price
Out-of-the-money	Underlying market > strike price

TABLE 1.4 Moneyness and Spot when Selling Binaries

Moneyness	Relationship to Spot
In-the-money	Underlying market > strike price
At-the-money	Underlying market = strike price
Out-of-the-money	Underlying market < strike price

When buying a binary option, remember these relationships between moneyness and the underlying market price.

In-the-money status for the seller is different (Table 1.4). Being ITM for sellers means they are betting that the underlying spot price is less than the binary option strike price. The binary contract should be seen as a floor that the spot falls through. That is what the seller wants to see happen. Therefore the premium for that strike price increases for those who want to trade with the downward momentum. Remember, at Nadex the premium for selling is $100 − bid.

The trader receives the bid price and keeps it if the settlement price stays below the strike price.

For example, if the bid price is $85 for a binary option strike price, it means that the binary option strike price is deep-in-the-money for buyers, but deep-out-of-the-money for sellers. The market thinks there is an 85 percent probability of the spot price staying above the binary, but only a 15 percent probability of the spot price falling below the binary. If the market becomes bearish, the bid would decline. For example, the bid may be at $85 and then bearish news causes the bid to go down to $50. The trader betting on a fall of the spot would pay $100 − bid or $50, much higher than the $15 before.

Generally, a trader who is bearish and looking to an ITM binary option strike price would be looking at the bids being lower than $50. Following this logic, a very optimistic bearish market would have a very low price for the bid and asks. Ask prices of $10 for a binary option strike price is a very cheap option because the market is giving a low probability to the binary option settling in-the-money at expiration and paying $100. For traders looking at OTM strategies, they are betting that the opinion pool represented by the bid/ask range is wrong, and this kind of OTM trade provides a huge reward of 10:1 for being on the side of surprise.

We can affirm an extremely interesting relationship in the bid and ask price ranges between the bid and ask prices and market sentiment. Since the binary options pay only, at maximum, $100 when the binary option trade settles in-the-money, we can interpret the bid and ask prices as a sentiment probability. In effect, if the ask price is $80, the "crowd" is assigning an 80 percent probability that the option will work out.

If the bid price is $20, the market is, in effect, assigning an 80 percent probability that the binary option for a seller will work out. This is the exact inverse of the buying probability. Think about this a bit further. Binary option bid/ask pricing becomes a trader scorecard of the battle between buyers and sellers. It's the best real-time measure of bullish or bearish sentiment.

The challenge for the trader becomes one of knowing when to go with the crowd or against the crowd. Expected probabilities that the underlying market will reach or not reach a strike price are derived from bid and ask pricing. It is definitely predictive in value, but it is certainly only a conditional probability. This is because markets can and do change and react to new information. Ultimately, the status that is important is the value at settlement time. In the case of binary options, we have only one of two outcomes: $100 per unit or $0 per unit.

The Role of a Market Maker

The binary option trading is not an automatic match between buyers and sellers. There is another component to the process: the *market maker*. A market maker provides the liquidity. The essential role of the market maker is in fact to make the market. As familiarity with the binary option product increases, more market makers will be attracted to the opportunity. But let's get a deeper look at how the market maker fulfills his duty. Nadex has an agreement with Market Risk Management (MRM), which is an entity of IG Group, to price all markets on the Nadex exchange. But there should be no doubt that Nadex and IG are, in fact, taking the opposite position of the trader. In contrast, Cantor, NYSE, and CBOE are true exchanges and do not take the other side. This is a great advantage to the trader. However, the disadvantage is the potential lack of liquidity, if market makers are few or not providing pricing for the different binary options.

Let's understand further the role of market making with the binary options. John Austin, a former market maker and one of the originators of the binary option product, describes market making from his vantage point. He provided the following point of view:

> We need to begin with the traders. One trader looks at a price and wants to buy, while another trader looks at the same contract and wants to sell.

For example, the market maker makes a price at 48–51.

In a perfect world, two individual traders see the price and trade at the same time. One thinks the price is too high and goes short in one lot at a price of 48. The other thinks the price is too low and goes long in one lot at a price of 51. Both traders wait until expiration, and do not trade again, and neither does anyone else.

In this perfect world, the market maker has fulfilled his duty (that is, he has put liquidity onto the exchange and provided a tradable price for traders who don't want to work an order but would rather trade right away), but has left himself with absolutely no exposure to the final expiration level. He has bought one lot from the selling trader at 48 and sold one lot to the buying trader at 51, making a three-point profit for himself, regardless of where the market settles. This three-point profit is his reward for posting prices and taking risk.

In the real world, individual traders rarely choose to trade in opposite directions in identical sizes at the same time (if they did, there would be no need for market makers). In the real world, the market maker posts a price that may start at 48–51 before moving smoothly to, say, 78–81 and then dropping suddenly to, say, 19–22 and so on. Buyers and sellers come along more or less at random, buying or selling on the market maker's price in different sizes at different times. When the market maker sees a whole bunch of people buying a certain price he may tweak his price upward by a point or two to encourage some sellers to enter the market and balance his risk. Alternatively, a whole bunch of people selling a certain price may cause the market maker to tweak his price downward by a point or two to encourage some balancing buyers.

In practice, market makers are rarely able to balance their book perfectly, and end up wearing a position until expiration. So on any one expiration on any one contract, the market maker may make a large loss or a large profit.

But averaged over many contracts, over the course of a year, the effect of the market maker's spread should be to make the average price at which he buys from traders slightly lower than the average price at which he sells to traders. That is his reward for providing liquidity, and it is paid for by the fact that losing traders lose, over the course of a year, slightly more than winning traders win (because binary trading, like spot FX and all other derivatives trading, is a zero-sum game).

Understanding the role of market makers provides a better understanding of the real dynamics of binary option trading and why it is possible with honed trading skills to gain an edge in binary option trading and have winning bets. The actual bid and ask prices are not just the expected probabilities of bearish and bullish traders. It would be wrong and naive to interpret the bid and ask prices as a simple reflection of expected probabilities. The fact is that they also reflect adjustments the market makers make to encourage participation. The market maker wants more volume, because, over time, he will gain a fraction of the spread.

Market makers try to be quants and use option analytics to help determine adjustments in the bid and ask. But market making is not pure calculation. Matt Brief, the current market maker for IG Markets on the binaries, provided the following answer to a question on the use of some advanced analysis in regard to binary option pricing:

> **Question:** Do you actually consider the presence of volatility smiles in the case of currencies, and if so, do you calculate them? Related to this, do you look at risk reversals in your model as well?
>
> **Answer:** We try to keep our vols in line with the market. On the euro, for example, the market currently has a high implied vol on the downside (lower strikes), but on the upside (higher strikes), the implied vol is the same, or lower, than the ATM vol. So there is no volatility smile on the E/$ at present. We will tend to replicate this in our prices.

We can conclude that the actual bid and asks are not pure participant probabilities. Nor are they simply a function of some advanced formula or calculation engine, such as Black-Scholes, and so on. They reflect, instead, a combination of traders as well as market maker judgments and misjudgments! The fact is that market makers cannot estimate accurately the expected value of all strike prices, particularly those at the extremes, furthest away from the spot price. When this happens, they have to make a best guess and usually increase the ask price to protect against uncertainty. This suggests that traders should pay closer attention to strike prices or ladders that are deep-out-of-the-money, where there is lighter volume. In this out-of-the-money price zone, the bid and asks are not always directly reflective of the crowd, nor subject to the same quantitative rigor of trading prices associated with ATM and ITM binary options.

Are Premiums Fairly Priced?

Many traders will wonder whether the premiums (bid/asks) are fairly priced. They do not want to pay more than they have to. Markets, when working efficiently, should result in option premiums that are fairly valued. So let's look at a comparison of the bid and ask pricing at Nadex with an advanced option calculator. Do we get similar premiums? If not, why are there differences? By entering the key pricing information in the calculator supplied by Superderivatives, a world-class professional derivative option calculator, the result was different from the real-time Nadex premium pricing of the AUD/USD weekly 1.065 binary contract (Table 1.4), which shows a bid of 16 and an ask of 21.5.

In contrast to the Nadex real-time pricing, the Superderivatives engine using the same expiration date (April 15, 2011) and binary strike price for the AUD/USD (1.6025) showed a bid/ask range of 7.75/19.75. At that same moment, the same binary strike price on the Nadex platform showed a bid/ask of 16/21.5.

Why might there be a difference between the Nadex pricing and the calculations of advanced option-pricing engines such as Superderivatives or Bloomberg? The difference between what the option calculator shows and what is traded is attributed to volume and judgments of the market makers. *The main point here is that there is no true trade price.* It is, rather, a combination of supply and demand as well as the perceptions and misperceptions of the market maker who participates in providing liquidity.

Another example verifying mispricing in the bid and ask of Nadex is an analysis provided by the use of Mathematica's powerful option analysis engine. The bid/ask prices of the EUR/USD weekly binaries for a sample moment in time (June 28 at 9:25 A.M.) was processed using Mathematica software. According to Michael Kelly, Mathematica trainer and consultant, the results reported that: "Considering that the first two are overpriced, the third at 1.4375 is correctly priced and that from the fourth to the last are underpriced."

The main conclusion is that there is significant mispricing in these binary options. The implication for the average trader is that human judgment still dominates the binary option pricing. The bid/ask prices are simply reflections of error-prone opinions and the expectations of traders (see Table 1.5). The trader has the opportunity to profit from these conditions.

TABLE 1.5 Bid/Ask Comparative Pricing

Contract	Expiration	Bid
AUD/USD > 1.065 (3 p.m.)	15-APR-11	16

Binary Option Non-Laddered Trading

In contrast to Nadex, IG, Cantor, and NYSE, most binary option trading is done in non-laddered platforms. The trading is simpler and the choice traders make is whether the underlying market will be above or below, higher or lower at expiration time, than the price when the trader puts on the trade. Buying a call or put is also often the names of the trading actions. The payoff is usually around 80 percent profit. The risk is the amount put on the trade. *A key feature of these non-laddered binaries is the inability to exit a position.* Once the position is put on, one cannot close the positions. This is in contrast to the laddered binaries. The trader of these platforms also has risk of receiving inaccurate prices. The fact is that binary option firms offering non-laddered options do not have price transparency. The settlement prices for binary expirations will differ among different firms.

The challenge to the trader in these non-laddered binaries is to first reach a breakeven performance result. Traders around the world favor the very short-term expirations such as one minute. This is because they offer nearly instant results and satisfaction, thereby appealing to the gambling tendencies of those traders. Longer-term expirations above 15 minutes allow the trade to apply technical and fundamental analysis to the position and reduce or gain an edge as a result.

CHAPTER 2

Identifying Profit Return Potential in Binary Option Trading

There are many reasons to participate in binary option trading. First, it is challenging. It doesn't matter what background or profession you may have, binary option trading levels the playing field to all who seek to master it. This may be disappointing to some traders who have had great success in their own fields, only to find that the market doesn't care at all. Whether you are a doctor, lawyer, engineer, homemaker, truck driver, pilot, soldier, and so on, binary option trading will demand all of your skills, as well as your emotional intelligence. It is also exciting, as it provides quick feedback on whether your trades are right or wrong. Yet, the dominant reason is that binary option trading offers profitable trading opportunities at frequencies and magnitudes rarely seen in other markets. This chapter provides a review of what the profit potential can be in the laddered binary option trading.

Expected Probabilities

We can start from a basic description of the unique property of the laddered binary option. It is a fixed payoff of $100 per unit. This means that at any point in time, the value of the ask price would never be more than $100. As a result, we can derive the important outcome that is referred to as an expected probability. The easiest way to derive at an expected probability is to look at the ask price. The ask price can be seen as an approximate measure of what the market believes is the probability of success. A $50 USD ask price translates into an expected probability of 50 percent that the binary will settle above the strike price associated with the binary. An $80 USD ask price can be interpreted as an 80 percent expected probability. Whether one is trading a weekly binary option or an intraday option, at any given moment, the bid/ask range signals can be considered expectations of the market. The bid and ask prices represent a kind of crowd-mind that expresses the emotions of the market. It becomes a probability barometer measuring market opinion. These emotions become translated into the premiums paid for different strike prices. This aspect of the binary option market is perhaps its most profound feature.

Whether trading the Nadex, IG, Cantor, or NYSE binaries, the trader has a choice to follow or fade the crowd opinion. If the trader is bullish on the market and agrees with the emotions expressed in the ladder ask prices, he would buy a binary with an ask price of greater than 50. The larger the ask price, the greater the opinion of the trading community is that the price of the underlying market will be above the strike price. So, an ask price of 80 translates into 80 percent expected probability that the price will be above the binary strike price that is receiving the 80 ask. Conversely, a 20 ask translates into 80 percent of the trader crowd believes that the price will be below that associated ask price.

A good idea is to relate the expected probabilities to the degree to which the underlying market has to move to win or lose the positions.

We can see in Table 2.1 an example of various expected probabilities appearing, offering a range of probabilities at the start of a week. These strike prices were taken on a Monday morning for end-of-week expirations. A useful metric is to detect a strike price's percentage distance from the underlying spot market. We can see that an ask price of 81.5 converts to a percentage distance of 1.4 percent from the underlying spot. This means the market has to move down more than 1.4 percent from the spot. The trader needs to decide if this is a reasonable expectation that it would not do so in order to win.

While there is no guarantee that the expected probability will turn out to be settling at $100, scanning the offer ask prices provides a good first approximation of market opinion. Once a scan of market expectations is done, the next step is deciding on the direction of your binary trade. Do you want to join the crowd or do you want to be contrarian? Do you want a high return with a lower chance of winning versus a lower return with a high chance of

TABLE 2.1   Sample Distribution of Expected Probabilities from 25 to 81 Percent on December 14, 2015, Expiring December 18, 2015

Date	Bid	Ask	Binary Option Contract (Indicative Price)
12/14/15	75	81.50	EUR/USD > 1.0825 (1.09847)
12/14/15	65	69.50	GBP/USD > 1.5075 (1.51537)
12/14/15	52.25	58.25	AUD/USD > 0.7225 (0.7243)
12/14/15	40	46.25	USD/CAD > 1.3775 (1.3738)
12/14/15	36	42.50	EUR/JPY > 133.25 (132.74)
12/14/15	18.25	25	GBP/JPY > 184.75 (183.144)

winning? A binary trade costing $20 per unit and paying off $100 results in a 5:1 return (excluding fees).

While this is a great result for any particular trade, the ultimate test is the profitability curve that results over time. Simple mathematics shows that a 5:1 binary option reward/risk ratio is required to be profitable in the long run—at least one win over every five trades. One trade, costing $20, turning out to be a winner will result in an $80 profit. The next four trades can be losers and the total result would be breakeven. In contrast, an $80 cost for a binary trade indicates a market expectation of an 80 percent probability of being a winner. One loser would result in an $80 loss, and would require four winners in the next five trades to get to breakeven. One has to be more than 80 percent accurate to go with a deep-in-the-money strategy, buying $80 binary contracts. In fact, no matter what win/loss ratio a trader has, the challenge for the trader will be to avoid having one loss risk wiping out a large winning streak!

Winning Occurrence Analysis

Which binary option strike prices are more likely to win? Conducting an occurrence analysis test demonstrated the attractiveness of binary option trading as a route to profitability. During the sample week of January 10 to 14, using an algorithm search function that retrieved all offer prices, the algorithm was instructed to find a trade that had a market probability of 80 percent for long positions, and 20 percent for short positions. Both directions had the same expected probabilities. The result was 87 trades and a 14.6 percent return for the week (see Table 2.2).

TABLE 2.2 Same Occurrence Analysis

Strategy	Buy Binary Contracts > 80 and Sell Contracts < 20
Number of trades	87
Capital committed for long positions	$3,121
Capital committed for shorting positions	$330
Return results	409.25
Return on weekly investment	14.66%

Even more interesting is the fact that a strategy that was buy everything over 80 percent, resulting in a win for a $100 payout, worked very well. This doesn't mean that this strategy will work all the time. Markets can suddenly shift their sentiment and have surprise reversals. Binary option traders always using a pure strategy have to be prepared for setbacks.

In another sample test, how would a strategy focusing on deep-out-of-the-money trading work? During the same sample period of January 10 to 14, 19 binary option strike prices were traded. Deep-out-of-the-money (less than 50 percent probability) positions were bought. If there were deep-in-the-money positions (over 75 percent probability), they were sold. They were held not for a whole week but only one to three days. The percentage returns had some losses, but were offset by very large gains using the combined strategy of deep-out-of-the-money trading (Table 2.3).

In reviewing Table 2.4, we can obtain a greater sense of the distribution of expected probabilities that the binary options markets generate during a week. The table presents a snapshot of the probabilities at about 10 A.M. every morning during a sample week (May 16 to 20, 2011) for different probability ranges. For example, on Monday, there were 30 binary option contracts with an ask price between $10 to 20. Of these 30 contracts, only one resulted in-the-money at the Friday expiration. In contrast, for the cohort of $45 to 55 for ask prices on Monday, there were 15 contracts. Of these, nine settled in-the-money at expiration on Friday. That represents a 60 percent success rate. Even more interesting is the fate of the 42 contracts that were deep-in-the money on Monday ($75 to $90). Of these 42, all of them were winners.

This is only a one-week sample, but it is instructive regarding the potential of winning outcomes and the challenges. In this single week, the at- or near-the-money strategies had the highest winning percentage.

TABLE 2.3 Deep-Out-of-the-Money Sample Results

Underlying	Strike	Initial Price	Closing Price	Direction	Days Held	Return %	Return ($s)
USD/CAD	0.9925	$23.50	$84.50	Long	2	259.60%	$61.00
USD/CAD	0.9825	$83.00	$90.50	Short	2	–9.00%	($7.50)
USD/CHF	0.9875	$22.00	$15.00	Long	1	–31.80%	($7.00)
USD/CHF	0.9975	$12.50	$8.00	Long	1	–36.00%	($4.50)
EUR/USD	1.3025	$34.00	$96.00	Long	3	182.40%	$62.00
EUR/USD	1.3125	$24.00	$94.50	Long	3	293.80%	$70.50
EUR/USD	1.3225	$12.50	$84.00	Long	2	572.00%	$71.50
GBP/USD	1.5525	$53.00	$83.00	Long	1	56.60%	$30.00
GBP/USD	1.5725	$56.50	$72.00	Long	1	27.40%	$15.50
USD/JPY	82.25	$71.50	$77.00	Short	1	–7.70%	($5.50)
USD/JPY	82.25	$45.00	$39.00	Long	1	–13.30%	($6.00)
Crude Oil	90.25	$35.50	$73.00	Long	3	105.60%	$37.50
Copper	438.50	$30.00	$60.00	Long	2	100.00%	$30.00
S&P 500	1287.50	$23.00	$31.00	Long	1	34.80%	$8.00
Gold	1388.50	$26.00	$45.50	Long	2	75.00%	$19.50
Silver	2825	$90.00	$26.50	Short	3	70.60%	$63.50
Silver	2825	$37.50	$60.00	Long	1	60.00%	$22.50
Silver	2975	$26.50	$5.00	Long	2	–81.10%	($21.50)
DAX	7075	$34.00	$39.50	Long	1	16.20%	$5.50
					Total Returns	60.10%	$445.00

A good way to look at the expected probabilities of the binary contracts in Table 2.4 is to view them as horses in a race. Each probability range (that is, 10–20 percent, and so on), as depicted in Table 2.6, represents an opportunity to get to the finish line of 100 percent by the end of the week. But in this kind of horse race, the trader is the jockey, and the racetrack conditions can change any minute. Another difference is you can switch horses in the middle of the race!

TABLE 2.4 Binary Option Contract Buying Probabilities

	16-May	17-May	18-May	19-May	20-May	ITMM	(ITMW)		
	MON	TUE	WED	THUR	FRI		%ITM	ITM	%ITM
10–20	30	30	25	16	8	1	3	1	4
20–30	24	23	19	11	5	2	8	4	21
30–40	18	21	14	10	5	5	28	2	14
45–55	15	18	11	11	4	9	60	8	73
55–75	30	29	24	15	9	25	30	19	79
75–90	42	38	32	22	10	42	23	32	100
Total Contracts	159	159	125	85	41				

Identifying Potential Profits in High-Low Binaries

In contrast to the laddered binaries, let's consider binary trading on platforms that offer trade decisions that the underlying markets will be higher or lower at expiration. They do not provide inherent expected probabilities. In effect, these trades are at-the-money trades and have a theoretical probability of 50 percent. Traders at these binaries do not get information on the opinion of the crowd of traders from these platforms.

The challenge for the binary option trader using non-laddered binaries is to identify high probable trading signals. Keep in mind that binaries that require a higher or lower trading decision is essentially a momentum directional decision. The strongest signal that is available for this kind of trading is a break in a pattern. Therefore, choosing to enter on a break and then picking an appropriate duration for the trade are the two key factors for successful trading of the high-low binaries.

Each trader needs to fine-tune the combination of expirations and what the best chart time frame to use (Table 2.5). The following combinations, however, are a useful place to start.

TABLE 2.5   Matching Charts with Durations

Expiration Duration	Best Chart to View
1 Min	1-Minute Renko Charts
5 Min	1-Minute Three-Line Break Charts
15 Min	15-Minute Candlestick
End of Day	30-Minute Three-Line Break
End of Week	1-Day Three-Line Break

TIP

Predicting the direction of the market is a key to binary option trading, but many traders ignore that predicting where the market will not go back to is also a high-payoff strategy. This strategy works well because the crowd energy pushing a price up or down quickly needs time to rest and new information is necessary to reverse the situation.

CHAPTER 3

Sentiment Analysis: New Predictive Tools

This chapter provides an introduction and guide to one of the recent, and increasingly important tool for understanding fundamental forces that relates to binary option trading. Let's call it *sentiment detection* for predicting direction. You will learn how to create and use your own sentiment detection tools as part of conducting fundamental analysis. A review of key fundamental economic forces and which markets they affect are also provided.

Defining Sentiment

At the heart of binary option trading is the need to anticipate the direction the underlying market will go. To make that decision, traders cannot ignore market sentiment. But the question arises: Just what is market sentiment? For starters, a text-mining technical definition of *sentiment* is this: *the orientation (or polarity) of the opinion on the subject that deviates from the neutral state* (Yi and Niblack 2005). In other words, sentiment relating to market conditions refers to whether opinion is positive or negative. So how can traders detect it? All of us are familiar with viewing the market as if it was a biological sentient being that has moods. Take, for instance, when the market is referred to as nervous or optimistic—these descriptions underscore our tendency to anthropomorphize the market. When it comes down to shaping trades, and in particular shaping binary option trades, the trader needs new and sharper tools to trace the shape of market sentiment. The fact is that now all trading is, in this age of the Internet, a social web phenomenon. "Studies of contagion share the finding that people's feelings and behaviors are strongly affected by their observations of others" (Olson 2006).

The Internet has had a fantastic impact on trading because it acts as a medium propagating a wave. The wave in trading is the collective grouping of emotions. It is similar to what computational chemistry calls *crowd-minds*. According to a recent work on artificial chemistry titled *Dynamics of Crowd-Minds* (Adamatzky 2005), "A crowd-mind emerges when formation of a crowd causes fusion of individual minds into one collective mind. Members of the crowd lose their individuality. The deindividualization leads to derationalization: emotional, impulsive, and irrational behavior."

The emergence of the Internet is producing new sets of tools that can be put to effective use by the binary option trader. The new set of tools that can be put to effective use by the trader is called *text mining*. Text mining is the art and science of finding word trends in a given document. The goal is to determine and categorize the meaning of those documents and text. Related to text mining is sentiment analysis. Here is how a leading sentiment scientist described the field (Xiaoxu, Huizhen, and Jingbo 2010):

> With the rapid growing availability of opinion-rich resources on the Internet such as product reviews, blogs and twitters, sentiment analysis becomes a popular research direction whose goal is to determine public assessments on products or social issues. Polarity analysis is one of fundamental techniques in sentiment analysis. To determine the polarity expressed by an opinionated sentence, it is important to first determine which words have sentiment tendency (i.e., positive or negative), referred to as sentiment word identification. A sentiment word is a word that can express positive or negative feelings of the opinion holder.

Text mining is quickly becoming a key part of our lives. In fact, almost everyone has experienced text mining—simply by using an Internet search engine. With advances in programming and technology, text mining will generate an entire new set of tools for detecting sentiment and it will revolutionize technical analysis. At its most basic, the search engine scans documents, web pages, blogs, or anything else that has text and shows you where to find them. In the language of experts, these are called keyboard Boolean searches. The results are often ambiguous and inaccurate.

Of course, the challenge of text searching goes beyond the retrieval of information. With *trillions* of words on the Internet, search engines need to instantly scan sites and convert that information into something useful. The software powering the searches use specialized programs called algorithms, or algos, to zero in on the data.

Google has mastered search engine algorithms, constantly tweaking them to produce even better results. But text mining goes way beyond looking up something online. Almost all business sectors can utilize this technology.

For example, text mining is penetrating call rooms and customer service functions—making it faster and easier to handle questions and complaints. Reuters and Dow Jones are also developing text mining applications. And, of course, financial markets are just beginning to look at text mining. The field of text mining is evolving quickly with many new companies offering text search and semantic analysis services. Open source software such as GATE (http://gate.ac.uk) that processes text is now fully developed and available to anyone. This software enables the ability to scan, retrieve, annotate text, and identify concepts (see the sidebar for more information).

WHAT IS GATE?

GATE is the acronym for general architecture for text engineering. Professor Ronen Feldman, co-founder and chief scientist of Digital Trowel, has been a leader in applying text mining and sentiment analysis to financial markets. His case studies tracked sentiment changes in stocks for their predictive value. Does a change in sentiment predict a change in stock price direction? His work is discovering that it can be predictive (see more details at www.digitaltrowel.com). At this time, text-mining tools are still focused on a single stock rather than a sector. To have effective predictive results for a sector, a lot more work has to be done to retrieve the right documents. If one wanted opinion about the gold sector, just searching for gold would bring in many other unrelated documents. When a search retrieves unrelated results, the effect is similar to a low signal/noise ratio in physics. Special algorithms in these situations are needed to disambiguate the results.

Others in the financial industry are applying text search tools to Twitter and other social media to profile mood changes. Research is ongoing on how to use Twitter as a source of sentiment that has predictive value. A recent study focused on using Twitter to predict next-day pricing of the S&P 100. "We collected the tweets via Twitter's REST API for streaming data using symbols of the Standard and Poor's 100 stocks (S&P 100) as keywords. In this study, we focus only on predicting the S&P 100). The time period of our dataset is between Nov. 2, 2101, and Feb. 7, 2013, which gave us 624,782 tweets." They developed in their methodology a ratio of positive/negative opinion words per day. They concluded:

> Predicting the stock market is an important but difficult problem. This paper showed that Twitter's topic-based sentiment can improve the prediction accuracy beyond existing non-topic based approaches. (Si, Mukherjee, Liu, Li, Li, and Deng 2013, 28)

The challenge for usefully using Twitter as a crowd sourcing and sentiment prediction tool for trading is rooted in the problem of sampling misrepresentation. Sampling Twitter followers would be very inaccurate as a predictor without knowing who the Twitter users are and whether they are representative of the overall population of traders. To be statistically reliable and effective, Twitter data needs a lot of post-monitoring processing. At best, Twitter-sentiment-based indicators would be a confirming indicator. (See the site http://twittersentiment.appspot.com/, which takes a snapshot of Twitter opinion.)

While the overall field of text searching for understanding the mood of the market is getting better, the goal is to actually use the information to help the trader. A next step would be to match the sentiment scans with price action.

Text Mining Mood on the U.S. Dollar

Let's look at an example involving the U.S. dollar index and the potential for using text mining as a predictive tool.

SentiMetrix, a text-mining firm, conducted a test scan from April 17 to May 15 of the Internet for sentiment on the U.S. Dollar Index. It showed some promise (Figure 3.1). During a test period, the Internet was scanned for mentions of the U.S. Dollar Index and then using natural language processing (NLP), the documents were evaluated (not by humans) for emotional tags regarding the U.S. dollar. The result was a sentiment polarity index. While this is a small sample of one week, it demonstrates that opinion mining regarding the U.S. dollar is possible and that certainly we can detect shifts in positive and negative attitudes for the U.S. dollar. An improved approach would be to generate a scan at a regular interval during the week and then match the sentiment score to price action. Much more work

FIGURE 3.1   U.S. Dollar Index versus Sentiment Score

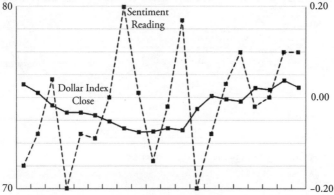

Source: Sentiment analysis data provided by SentiMetrix, Inc. Used with permission.

needs to be done to achieve predictive accuracy, but the goal of building sentiment-leading indicators is worthy and exciting and rapidly gaining in effectiveness.

In another example of matching sentiment against price action we can see how positive and negative sentiment regarding crude oil correlates with price action (Figure 3.2). News, blogs, video, and forums over the Internet were scanned during the week of May 28 to June 9 on sentiment regarding crude oil prices. Each day's negative scores were converted into a line graph and overlaid against each day's positive scores. Then the actual Brent crude oil prices were matched against these negative and positive lines. While this is only a sample period, we can see that it is worthwhile to use sentiment data as a gauge for price direction. A peak in negative sentiment on crude oil occurred on May 31 as crude oil prices reached a high of 102.98. It was followed by decline in crude oil prices. Sentiment reached a bottom negative score on June 5 and positive sentiment started bouncing up. Crude oil prices rose back to the 102 area a few days later. While the data needs much more granularity, we can sense, even at this early stage in the art and science of sentiment-based signals that there are two key areas that will be useful to the trader. First, when positive or negative sentiment crosses over, the trader can use this as a clue that market opinion is shifting. It also appears that sentiment peaks, whether positive or negative, are the key milestones relating to subsequent price changes and offer great potential as a source of trading signals.

FIGURE 3.2   Negative and Positive Sentiment and Crude Oil Prices

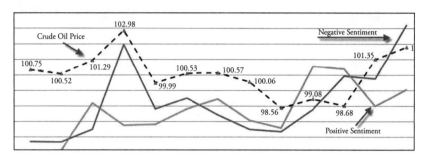

The state of text mining is already evolving to a brand new level. The first step was just grabbing words and counting them or transforming the document into a statistical breakdown of sorts. It's now at a point at which millions of documents can be scanned virtually in seconds with a state-of-the-art text retrieval system. But until machines can do natural language processing at the level of humans, it will be up to the trader to initiate and complete the task of sentiment mining. Let's see how any trader can apply this new technology every day to binary option trading.

The field of text mining sentiment continues to rapidly evolve approaches to market prediction. A recent study (Wong, Liu, and Chiang 2014) reports the development of an algorithm based on news articles. Here is what they did.

> We identified 553 stocks that were traded from 1/1/2008 to 9/30/2013 and listed in at least one of the S&P 500, DJIA, or Nasdaq stock indices during that period. We then downloaded opening and closing prices[2] of the stocks from CRSP.[3] Additional stock information was downloaded from Compustat. For text data, we downloaded the full text of all articles published in the print version of WSJ in the same period. We computed the document counts per day that mention the top 1,000 words of highest frequency and the company names of the 553 stocks. After applying a stoplist and removing company names with too few mentions, we obtained a list of 1,354 words.

It should yield results of better than 55.7 percent accuracy for predicting daily price movements (Wong, Liu, and Chang 2014).

TIP

Read *Sentiment Analysis: Mining Opinions, Sentiments, and Emotions* by Bing Liu

Traders with experience in programming can actually do their own text mining and twitter mining. Using the open source programming called R, one can extract tweets and measure the sentiment in those tweets (see Zhao 2015).

For those who want a program that does the text mining, see www.attensity .com; Feinerer, Hornik, and Meyer 2008; and Moujahid 2014.

Applying Your Own Sentiment Detection When Trading Binaries

The first step is to decide on what market sentiment the trader wants to tag or monitor. What emotion is being expressed relating to a particular market? This is where the rubber meets the road. The technology of text searches at this point is still a dumb technology. The search function is extremely fast in retrieving documents, but it is not that smart at filtering out the noise. A lot of unrelated documents get retrieved. This is because the Internet is full of unstructured text. It is a bag of words that has to be categorized.

So the binary option trader is really more advanced than the search engine, at least at specifying what to look for so the search engine retrieves the right documents. This is called *semantic processing*. In February 2011, IBM demonstrated a breakthrough in semantic processing and text search when Watson won a contest on the TV show *Jeopardy*. Watson, as you may recall, is the name of the IBM computer system that competed against two human competitors on *Jeopardy*. The breakthrough was that Watson wasn't just searching its memory banks for keywords—it also had to understand how the words related to one another. In this era of Watson, computer programs will be important assistants in opinion mining and, as a result, it will mean any person is able to quickly understand the mood of the market. Until then, the trader has to do the work of a future Watson. But it can and should be done for binary option trading. Here is how. It is not that hard to do (Figure 3.3).

FIGURE 3.3 Risk Appetite/Risk Aversion Search Phases

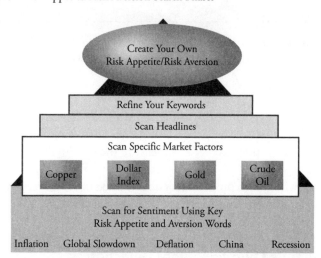

Let's explore each key step on how any trader can apply sentiment detection tools.

Step 1: Use Key Terms — Risk Appetite and Risk Aversion

A basic understanding of market forces generates the realization that there are two major emotional forces that become expressed in the market. Those forces are market moods on *risk appetite* and *risk aversion*. You can consider them the major axis of sentiment. However, don't attribute negative or positive associations with either term. They are neither good nor bad. Using the words risk appetite and risk aversion helps describe where the crowd-mind of market opinion is clustering. These two opinion pools are always in flux.

In the new fundamentals, sentiment trumps economics in affecting price moves. This doesn't mean fundamentals don't count. It means that the market is not only an information engine generating valuation, it is also an expectation engine, spewing out emotions. The words "risk appetite" are code for market optimism, while risk aversions are code for market fear. Each week the balance between risk appetite and risk fear constantly shifts and a virtual war and struggle ensues for which force is dominant. The lingo of sentiment science calls the resulting shift of sentiment *sentiment polarity*. The balance of sentiment and stability will shape the direction and speed of price moves. The binary option trader making a decision on direction is, in a very real sense, measuring the emotions of the market. Weekly market direction reflects a precarious balance of fears. There are many fears and traders should become

FIGURE 3.4 Impact of High Growth

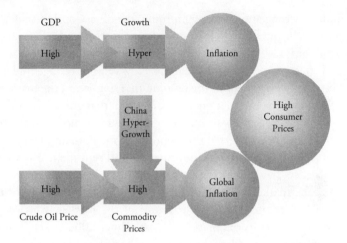

familiar with them. Fears shift from one polarity to the other and can do so very quickly. For example, if fear of inflation is dominant, market direction will tend to be bullish on commodity prices (Figure 3.4). Fear of U.S. deficits becomes a force reflecting bearish sentiment toward the U.S. dollar. Fear of Middle East instability, leads to price appreciation in crude oil. Fear of a China slowdown, can lead to a bearish view of the Australian dollar and fears of a global slowdown (see Figure 3.5).

FIGURE 3.5 Impacts of Slow Growth or Recession

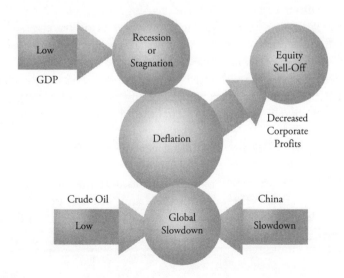

Step 2: Scan for Specific Fears

Every Sunday evening and Monday morning, the binary option trader should ask and answer the question: Which fears dominate the market this week? The answers will point to likely market directions. But how can the average trader quickly and effectively extract information? How can the average trader obtain accurate Internet searches about the opinion that dominates the markets? Fortunately, the rise of the Internet provides a medium that quickly transfers emotional information. Emotions spread like molecules in a medium, reactive and diffuse. Emotions are transferred throughout the medium and converted into opinions. The boundary between information and sentiment often becomes blurred. This effect has been described as part of a cycle of market information processing: "The market reports by the news services often consist of trading participants' perceptions and interpretations of the market, which are then fed back to the traders in the market" (Oberlechner 2004, 137). The task of binary option trader is to filter the enormous bag of words that populate the social media and come to some conclusion about the intensity of sentiment regarding the underlying markets. To accomplish this, the binary option trader has to become a *sentiment miner*. Don't let the term scare you away. In a very real sense we are all sentiment and opinion miners every time we use language.

Step 3: Scan Headlines

Could the average binary option trader use sentiment mining to help shape their trades? If so, what everyday tools can be used by the trader to accurately extract market sentiment? It turns out that anyone can become a good sentiment miner using a few tips. First, the challenge is to spot occurrences of key terms that are tagged to the fundamental forces being searched. The main idea is to find the right terms. This is known in sentiment science as *Adjective-Verb-Adverb (AVA) combinations* and using *opinion lexicon* (Qiu 2011).

Traders scanning the web often see frequent references to the terms fear and greed. But these terms are too coarse and do not offer the granularity needed by the trader to accurately sketch the vectors of market opinion. The task is to classify sentiment that better correlates to opinions about expected market direction. There are three major, general, directional sentiments that characterize market emotions: bullish, bearish, and neutral. But to be helpful to the trader on a timely basis, these classifications need to be further unpacked and detailed. The words "bullish" and "bearish" are still at too general a level. Being bullish or bearish is the result of a collection or the *balance of fears* that make traders bullish or bearish or ambivalent. To successfully extract information from the social media about these forces requires a greater level of precision in the use of keywords and efficiency in search and retrieval. The average individual does not have the more advanced text mining tools that are emerging. But some basic strategies are effective.

Overlooked by many traders is the value of scanning headlines. Headlines provide a sentiment activation frame to capture fundamental opinion. They are effective because they are constructed by opinion leaders as devices to attract readers. Headlines may not be accurate as to representing actual economic data, but they are effective strength-attribute indicators that show the pulse of opinion. Headlines trigger excitation waves that actually take the shape of a contagion. Particularly in this age of the Internet, headlines that appear and disappear throughout the day and night provide real-time samples of sentiment trends. One headline is often replicated throughout the Internet, acting as a signal amplifier of sentiment.

The headline effect was very powerful when the rating agency Standard & Poor's announced its review of the U.S. government debt rating. The headline was: *Standard & Poor's Puts "Negative" Outlook on U.S. Rating.* The headline triggered a big response throughout the market (Figure 3.6). The result was that gold hit new highs in response.

FIGURE 3.6   Gold Rises on S&P Ratings Headline

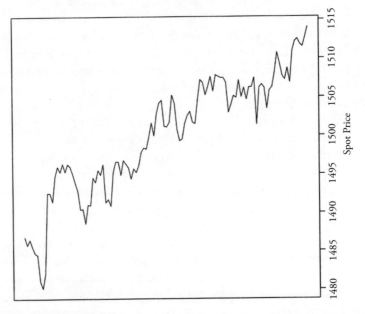

Source: Bloomberg Financial, L.P.

Step 4: Form Your Own Keywords for Search Retrieval

Beyond headlines, another critical tool in the hands of the binary trader are keywords. Monitoring keywords enables a quick test of the emotional strength of bullish and bearish sentiment on a 24/7 basis. While there are an enormous amount of keywords, there are certain words that enable a very effective sampling and mapping of the sentiment in the market. This is not a trivial task. But following the latest text mining strategies, the trick is to use words that are not subject to too much ambiguity and to filter out noise words that give no added value to the search (Qiu 2011).

Let's start with some initial suggested generic words that should be used. They are: "risk appetite," "risk aversion," "U.S. dollar," "Yellin," "Draghi," "deflation," "employment," "wages," and "inflation." These words are effective because they result in a high level of precision for retrieving the sentiment that the market is focused on. Think of each word as a landmark that is associated with an emotion. By using keywords, the trader is, in effect, doing shape science and finding the shape of sentiment. In the context of the science of sentiment analysis, the challenge of correctly matching keywords to the correct sentiment the words really reflect is called *sentiment polarity text classification*. The trader does not want to mismatch.

The words therefore have to have what is called *lexical cohesion*. Luckily, the use of words such as "risk aversion" and "risk appetite" have a high accuracy rate for retrieving and classifying the correct sentiment that goes with the word. The words also have to have an ability to link to emotions that can be categorized as positive and negative emotions. The positive emotions can also be broken down into "positive, no doubt"; "positive, doubt"; "negative, no doubt"; and "negative, doubt."

Let's apply this to the binary option trader scanning the web using keyword groups. Let's combine keywords with a set of verbs that are usually linked to emotions. For example, instead of the name of a key central banker (Yellen, Draghi, Carney (the trader can enter: "Yellen fears," or "Draghi fears" (Figure 3.7). Using the group of words "inflation fears" or "U.S. dollar fears" enables a quick grab of words relating to negative emotions about the dollar. The result is a greater detection of emotions. As a general rule, combine the name of a key leader with verbs such as "admits," "declares," "warns," "supports," "denies," and so on. The result is a retrieval of news that carries with it a lot of information about the emotions involved. A good idea for any trader would be to create his or her own table of opinion seed words, or a verbal quadrant.

These search strategies are flexible. It is a good idea to try different combinations to cast a wider net over the billions of words on the Internet. For example, the trader could try:

Central Banker + Adjectives
Yellen   = fears, hopes, declares

Entering each combination of words results in a slightly different grab, ensuring a wider and more diversified search. The effect is to provide a better match between the search and the retrieval of the emotion involved.

Once an underlying binary option market is chosen, word searches should become more targeted and specific. For example, if the currency pairs were the subject of binary option trades for the week, specific searches using the names of the key central bankers would be appropriate and effective. For every binary option market there are specific keywords that should be used. This is an area for which every trader can add his or her own creativity and improve his or her effectiveness by constructing his or her own dictionary of market emotions. Here are suggested words for use at any time for trying to gauge market sentiment. Start with any underlying market and add the suggested keywords using the different word combination formula (Figure 3.7).

FIGURE 3.7 U.S. Dollar Word Group

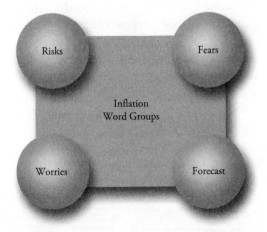

underlying market + risk appetite
underlying market + risk aversion
underlying market + fears
underlying market + optimism
underlying market + doubts
underlying market + pessimism
underlying market + deflation

We can generalize the entire search process in one equation or algorithm. It would be: underlying market + emotional adjective or adverb.

For example, for detecting U.S. dollar sentiment, a trader would generate a search, possibly using the group of words, at different times: U.S. Dollar Index risk appetite; U.S. Dollar Index risk aversion; U.S. Dollar Index fears; U.S. Dollar Index doubts; U.S. Dollar Index optimism. The result is an ability to count the positive and negative news items relating to the U.S. Dollar Index. This follows recent text mining and sentiment analysis methodology. Peter Hafez of RavenPack, referring to this methodology, states, "One may consider the sentiment ratio as the baseline for constructing market sentiment indices. As the ratio is measured as the count of positive to negative news items, it indirectly takes into consideration changes in news volume" (Hafez 2009).

Step 5: Create Your Own Risk Appetite/Risk Aversion Ranking

Since the words "risk appetite" and "risk aversion" are extremely effective as seed words to retrieve market sentiment, the trader should always conduct a general *risk appetite* and *risk aversion* search. By comparing the results of the search, the ratio between *risk appetite* and *risk aversion* beliefs can be approximated.

After retrieving the results of using *risk appetite* and *risk aversion,* the next step is to create your own sentiment ratio. The result is your own ability to give a thumbs-up or thumbs-down assessment about the mood of the market. The risk appetite/risk aversion ratio compares positive to negative sentiment results from your own text searches. This is a good technique—until special search engines can do a better job!

After doing a search for a good way to quantify the balance of risk appetite to risk aversion, you need to assign a number to the article or headline. Ask yourself: Is the article retrieved positive or negative about the underlying market? Keep score. This helps keep track of the strength of the sentiment. A useful technique is to use a ranking range of –5 to +5. If the total sum is positive, you have, in effect, a market that is risk positive.

GOOGLE TRENDS AND WORD CLOUDS

Social media is becoming a source for sentiment analysis and even basic search techniques and traders are beginning to use these tools to provide clues about the shape of opinion related to an underlying market. Two of the most recent tools are *Google Trends* and *Word Clouds*.

The millions of words in blogs, documents, and speeches form an unstructured bag that needs to be made sense of by the trader. An established method is called natural language processing to find patterns among the words. Word frequency analysis is particularly effective. Another technique is detecting the presence or absence of words. For example, when the Federal Open Market Committee (FOMC) issues a statement, any new phrase that occurs is carefully watched. What is really important is a statement or remark that occurs only one time. This is called a *hapax legomena* and in computer linguistics it is considered very significant. It is also significant when it occurs in financial statements. An example would be the word "deflation" suddenly appearing in a statement, but occurring only one time. It would set off market reactions. Word frequency counters are easily available and getting in the habit of conducting frequency analysis on key statements will help reinforce a trader's sense of the mood of the market.

Word clouds are also becoming popular and can become a very useful for traders. Word frequency should be considered a fundamental indicator about market mood and opinion. When applied correctly, they provide some additional perspective on changes in emphasis. They help the trader visualize what concerns the market at that moment. Here is a word cloud generated from the FOMC statement when they raised interest rates on December 16, 2015 (Figure 3.8). It clearly shows the focus on inflation rates as the key concern of the FOMC. That word appeared very prominently.

FIGURE 3.8 Word Cloud of FOMC Dec 16, 2015 Statement

In recent years, word cloud software has become multilingual, and even the Chinese trader can use word clouds to quantify sentiment. Traders can use several word cloud generators, such as *Wordle*, *Tagul*, and *WordItOut*. They are all accessible on the Internet.

References

Adamatzky, Andrew. 2005. *Dynamics of Crowd-Minds*. Singapore: World Scientific Publishing Company.

Guang, Qiu, Bing Liu, Jiajun Bu, and Chun Chen. 2011. "Opinion Word Expansion and Target Extraction through Double Propagation." *Computational Linguistics* 37 (1): 9–27. www.mitpressjournals.org/doi/pdf/10.1162/coli_a_00034.

Feinerer, Ingo, Kurt Hornik, and David Meyer. 2008. "Text Mining Infrastructure in R." *Journal of Statistical Software* 25(5): 1–54.

Hafez, Peter Ager. 2009. "Construction of Market Sentiment Indices Using News Sentiment." White Paper. RavenPack International S.L. (August 28): 3. http://ravenpack.com/research/indexsentpaperform.htm.

Miller, Rich. 2011. "Investors Favor Cash Over Commodities in Dim Poll Outlook." Bloomberg .com (May 12). www.bloomberg.com/news/2011-05-12/investors-shifting-to-cash-from-commodities-as-outlook-dims-in-global-poll.html.

Moujahid, Adil. 2014. "An Introduction to Text Mining using Twitter Streaming API and Python." July 21. http://adilmoujahid.com/posts/2014/07/twitter-analytics/.

Oberlechner, Thomas. 2004. *The Psychology of the Foreign Exchange Market*. Hoboken, NJ: John Wiley & Sons.

Olson, Kenneth R. 2006. "A Literature Review of Social Mood." *The Journal of Behavioral Finance* 7 (4): 193–203.

Pang, Bo, and Lillian Lee. 2008. "Opinion Minding and Sentiment Analysis." *Foundations and Trends in Information Retrieval* 2 (1–2): 1–135. www.cs.cornell.edu/home/llee/omsa/omsa.pdf.

Si, Mukherjee, Liu, Li, Li, and Deng. 2013. "Exploiting Topic-based Twitter Sentiment for Stock Prediction." http://www2.cs.uh.edu/~arjun/papers/stock_prediction_acl_13.pdf.

Xiaoxu, Fei, Huizhen Wang, and Jingbo Zhu. 2010. "Sentiment Word Identification Using the Maximum Entropy Model." Natural Language Processing and Knowledge Engineering (NLP-KE), 2010. International Conference (August): 1–4, 21–23. http://ieeexplore .ieee.org/xpl/freeabs_all.jsp?arnumber=5587811.

Yi, Jeonghee, and Wayne Niblack. 2005. "Sentiment Mining in WebFountain." http://suraj .lums.edu.pk/~cs631s05/Papers/sentiment_webfountain.pdf.

Wong, Felix Ming Fai, Zhenming Liu, and Mung Chiang. 2014. "Stock Market Prediction from WSJ: Text Mining via Sparse Matrix Factorization." http://arxiv.org/pdf/1406.7330.pdf.

Zhao, Yanchang. 2015. "Text Mining with R-Twitter Data Analysis." R and Data Mining Workshop, Deakin University, Melbourne. www.RDatamining.com.

CHAPTER 4

Tracking Fundamental Forces That Impact Markets

A Primer for Binary Traders

While finding the predominant sentiment for the markets is important for selecting the direction of trading in the coming week, basic fundamental economic forces also affect the movement of prices. These forces are often in the background, but remain important to monitor. The objective of this chapter is to provide a basic understanding of the fundamental forces that a binary option trader should know and track.

The relationship between economic fundamental forces and markets is not linear. This means that tomorrow's or next week's price direction is not directly predictable based on today's or yesterday's price patterns. Rather, price action is more chemical in nature, similar to what chemists refer to as a reaction-diffusion event, where an acid is dropped into a base and then the reaction follows a non-linear path. The globalization of the world economy promotes, of course, a gliding effect, in which a change in GDP growth, inflation, interest rates, employment, wage growth, housing prices, in one country, or market, generates ripples, and triggers a reaction and glides or cascades across the world. The gliding medium is the World Wide Web. A trigger event could be an earthquake, a sell-off in metals, a remark by a finance minister, or many other exogenous events. The fact is that there is no place to hide in the world economy. Once an event occurs, what is predictable is that there will be a reaction. The reaction varies in relationship to the level of surprise. Expectations therefore are itself a major fundamental force. After the reaction, the market digests the news and experiences a diffusion of original impact of the surprise.

The Fundamental Forces

The trader should now fear gaining knowledge about fundamental forces. Fortunately, we have filtered the key forces that shape market movements. Let's begin our tour of fundamental forces and relationships by reviewing the most global of all forces—China. We then review the impact of commodity markets, gold, the U.S. dollar, and other forces that need to be understood to build skills in trading binary options.

China and the Global Markets

There is no doubt that economic expectations on China's growth are and will increasingly become key drivers in the global economy. The importance of China in the world economy is partially reflected by the IMF granting reserve status to the Chinese currency, the yuan, on November 30, 2015. Clearly the Chinese economy is integrating into the global economy. The binary trader should recognize the impact of economic news coming from China. The binary option trader needs to monitor China economic news for a variety of reasons. China is the world's production hub. It imports resources and exports consumer products for the rest of the world. First, if growth in China is strong, it will directly affect the entire world economy. Some underlying markets are more directly affected by China's economic surprises than others. For example, China imports key resources from Australia and therefore trading the AUD/USD, and the copper binaries should be considered first when China economic data releases relate to these markets (Figure 4.1).

The selloff in the Shanghai market lead to "black" Monday on August 24, demonstrating how the sentiment of fear cascades through markets.

Secondly, when markets open Monday mornings in Asia, watching whether the Shanghai Index is bullish or bearish gives a powerful clue to which markets binary traders should focus on as the week opens. A classic example is the market actions in August 2015 (Figure 4.2) relating to China's devaluation of the yuan on August 11.

FIGURE 4.1   China Growth Expectations Affect Aussie and Copper Markets

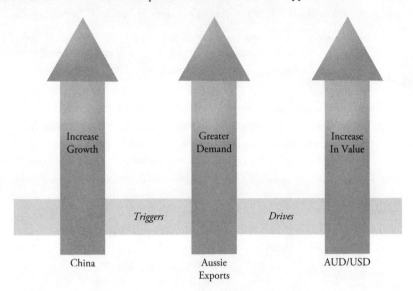

FIGURE 4.2   Shanghai Index Sell-Off and Fear Spreads to S&P 500

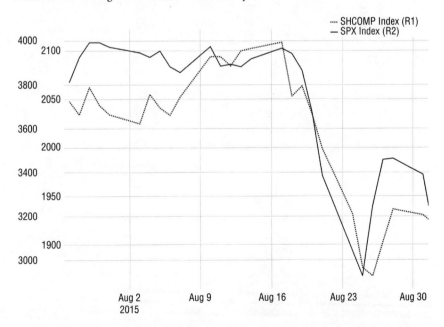

Trading China news is now possible at Nadex and IG by trading the China A50 and at IG the China CSI 300 Index. These provide weekly, daily, and intraday opportunities.

Global Growth and Commodity Markets

In reviewing global market conditions, the trader will notice that an over-arching theme is global growth and global slowdown. A good way to look at growth is to visualize it as a process of cause and effect. Global growth or expectations of growth (Figure 4.3) generate inflation, higher consumer prices, higher commodity prices, and increased interest rates. At some point, the increased interest rates start slowing down the growth to damper inflation.

In a scenario of a global slowdown, the key fundamental forces reverse. Low GDP expectations lead to lower demand for crude oil, lower commodity prices, and equity markets become less attractive. The big fear is no longer inflation, but deflation. The fear of deflation applies directly to the Eurozone and to Japan, both of which have had a difficult time generating growth. Traders need to monitor economic data releases on inflation in these countries to detect any changes in the potential for pushing prices higher.

FIGURE 4.3A   Global Growth Fundamental Factors

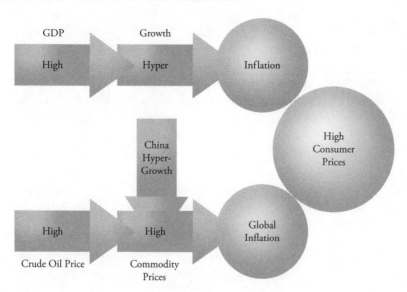

FIGURE 4.3B Global Slowdown Fundamental Factors

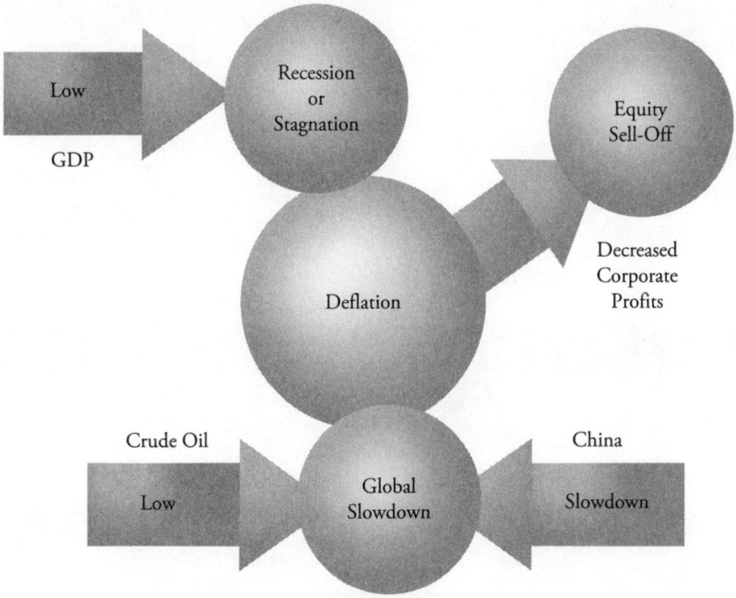

Commodity Markets as a Global Fundamental Force

Commodity markets will continue to be a valuable source for detecting profitable opportunities in binary option trading. A rise or fall in commodities should be used to select and shape binary option trades. Depending on the size of a move, a drop or spike in commodities spills over into the equity markets. The collapse of oil to historic lows during December 2015 is a case in point (Figure 4.4).

The binary trader looking to trade oil needs to understand and take a measure of the trend or pattern that is in place. After a surge down, the trader can try to join the sentiment and predict that oil will go further down. This requires good timing on choosing the expiration. However, it is more likely to predict that after a surge down crude oil will not likely bounce back. It will take a shift in global growth levels or a decline in oil production to be bullish on crude oil.

Beyond the overall fundamental forces, the binary option trader should track specific correlations between different markets and instruments. The value of being updated on correlations lies in reducing risk as well as augmenting profits. When trading several different underlying markets at one time, if two or more were highly correlated, the trader has the risk of incurring a loss in all those markets that are correlated. Of course, the potential of being correct increases and is augmented. Generally, reducing risk is achieved by trying to trade have less correlated markets during the trading period.

FIGURE 4.4   Collapse of Oil

Correlations and Co-Movement Useful for Trading Binary Markets

Let's review some important correlations and co-movements that binary traders ought to know. These include, but are not limited to: the Aussie dollar and copper, gold and the U.S. dollar, the USD/JPY and the S&P 500, as well as a set of fears that act as market forces.

China, the Shanghai Index, AUD/USD, and Copper

On August 11, 2015 China devalued the RMB and caused a major reaction in the Shanghai Index and subsequently in the S&P 500 index (Figure 4.5). The impact of China economic data on global markets is increasing and the binary trader should continue to play close attention to the Shanghai Index and the value of the Chinese yuan.

A correlation that should also not be ignored is the AUD/USD co-movements with copper (Figure 4.6).

Both the copper and the AUD/USD binaries can be treated as essentially trading the same event. Copper can be used as a directional indicator for strength or weakness in the Aussie and vice versa. We can see the close relationship between copper and the Aussie (Figure 4.6). There are times when the

FIGURE 4.5 Shanghai Sell Off in August 2015

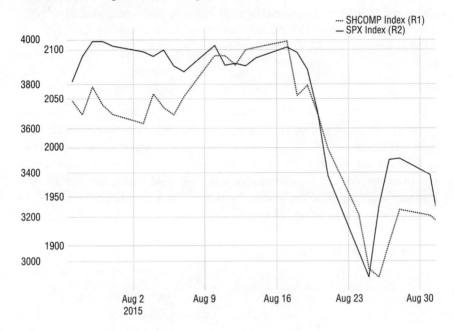

FIGURE 4.6 Copper and the Aussie

correlation between the AUD/USD and copper approaches over 90 percent, and there are times when the relationship hits a disconnect and there is no correlation. The trader should not take for granted a consistently high correlation between the AUD/USD and copper markets.

Gold

Gold is often treated as a risk-aversion basket, attracting capital in times of crises. It's important, though counter-intuitive, for the trader to realize that gold can be sold off if the crisis is so big that it requires the selling of gold to raise capital. Traders betting that gold will always rise in response to crises, therefore, have to be careful. Such rises in gold occur, but when it is a response to a crisis, it is likely to be temporary. Consider the gold movements in reaction to the Paris Terrorist attacks of November 14, 2015 (Figure 4.7).

FIGURE 4.7   Gold Rises in Response to Paris Terror Attacks

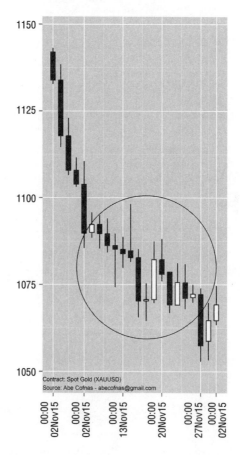

From a more macroeconomic and fundamental force perspective, gold acts as a hedge against inflation. Gold generally attracts capital when the market fears inflation or a major financial or global crisis. In recent years, inflation rates in the United States and globally has been well contained. The price of gold therefore declined in the context of a low-inflation world. Gold can attract capital when it is perceived as an asset that holds and increases value. When interest rates are expected to go up, money is attracted to where it will be making a greater return. That is why gold usually surges when there is surprise bad news on jobs (Figure 4.8). For example, on January 10, 2014, gold spiked up on a very bad NFP report.

Binary traders, after considering the fundamental expectations on interest rates, should always review the gold price pattern that is in force. This can be an intraday pattern. Is it going parabolic? Is it in a sideways range? Is it at key resistance or support levels?

FIGURE 4.8   Gold Bullish after Weak January 10 NFP Report

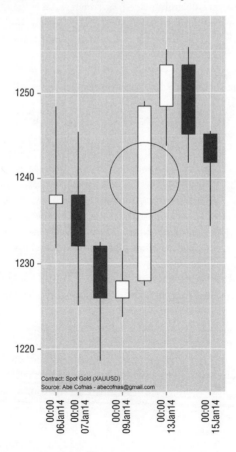

For the binary option trader in the coming years, the most important aspect in looking at the gold market is to assess whether interest rates are expected to move gradually or more aggressively. On December 16, 2015, the Federal Reserve increased interest rates 25 basis points. The statement they issued is very valuable to read carefully for insight on what the Federal Reserve monitors. Therefore, we are printing it in its entirety right here.

FOMC STATEMENT, DECEMBER 16, 2015

Information received since the Federal Open Market Committee met in October suggests that economic activity has been expanding at a moderate pace. Household spending and business fixed investment have been increasing at solid rates in recent months, and the housing sector has improved further; however, net exports have been soft. A range of recent labor market indicators, including ongoing job gains and declining unemployment, shows further improvement and confirms that underutilization of labor resources has diminished appreciably since early this year. Inflation has continued to run below the Committee's 2 percent longer-run objective, partly reflecting declines in energy prices and in prices of nonenergy imports. Market-based measures of inflation compensation remain low; some survey-based measures of longer-term inflation expectations have edged down.

Consistent with its statutory mandate, the Committee seeks to foster maximum employment and price stability. The Committee currently expects that, with gradual adjustments in the stance of monetary policy, economic activity will continue to expand at a moderate pace and labor market indicators will continue to strengthen. Overall, taking into account domestic and international developments, the Committee sees the risks to the outlook for both economic activity and the labor market as balanced. Inflation is expected to rise to 2 percent over the medium term as the transitory effects of declines in energy and import prices dissipate and the labor market strengthens further. The Committee continues to monitor inflation developments closely.

The Committee judges that there has been considerable improvement in labor market conditions this year, and it is reasonably confident that inflation will rise, over the medium term, to its 2 percent objective. Given the economic outlook, and recognizing the time it takes for policy actions to affect future economic outcomes, the Committee decided to raise the target range for the federal funds rate to 1/4 to 1/2 percent. The stance of monetary policy remains accommodative after this increase, thereby supporting further improvement in labor market conditions and a return to 2 percent inflation.

In determining the timing and size of future adjustments to the target range for the federal funds rate, the Committee will assess realized and expected economic conditions relative to its objectives of maximum employment and 2 percent inflation. This assessment will take into account a wide range of information, including measures of labor market conditions, indicators of inflation pressures and inflation expectations, and readings on financial and international developments. In light of the current shortfall of inflation from 2 percent, the Committee will carefully monitor actual and expected progress toward its inflation goal. The Committee expects that economic conditions will evolve in a manner that will warrant only gradual increases in the federal funds rate; the federal funds rate is likely to remain, for some time, below levels that are expected to prevail in the longer run. However, the actual path of the federal funds rate will depend on the economic outlook as informed by incoming data.

The Committee is maintaining its existing policy of reinvesting principal payments from its holdings of agency debt and agency mortgage-backed securities in agency mortgage-backed securities and of rolling over maturing Treasury securities at auction, and it anticipates doing so until normalization of the level of the federal funds rate is well under way. This policy, by keeping the Committee's holdings of longer-term securities at sizable levels, should help maintain accommodative financial conditions.

The word cloud shows that the important focus for the future of rate decisions will be on inflation rates (Figure 4.9).

FIGURE 4.9   Word Cloud of FOMC Dec 16 Statement

U.S. Dollar

The U.S. dollar is a generic term that is really an aggregate category and is quite vague. It has many references and associations. It needs to be disambiguated for it to be used by the binary option trader. An effective way to monitor U.S. dollar conditions and global sentiment regarding the U.S. dollar is to use the U.S. dollar index. It is an index that consists of several currencies in a basket and each component currency is given different weights. A common concern among traders is that this index is not really representative of global trade interactions. They are correct. A trade-weighted U.S. dollar index is more accurate and is used by the Federal Reserve and economists to evaluate the global strength of the dollar. But what is really important is that the U.S. dollar index is considered by the market to be an important indicator and therefore it has to be understood and monitored (Table 4.1).

Let's start with the U.S. dollar relationship with gold. They are inversely related most of the time. When gold goes up, the U.S. dollar goes down, and vice versa (Figure 4.10). The dollar acts as a haven basket in times of gold selloffs. Since the U.S. dollar index is not directly a binary option underlying market, the USD/CHF can be considered a good surrogate for playing this haven relationship (Figure 4.11). Also important to note is that the trader can use the exchange traded fund (ETF) UUP for tracking the U.S. dollar index (Figure 4.12). They are virtually identical and the added bonus is that the ETF UUP also offers option data to enable the trader to evaluate puts and calls on the UUP as a gauge on sentiment regarding the U.S. dollar.

TABLE 4.1 U.S. Dollar Index Components

Table Currency	Currency Weights %
Euro	57.6
Japanese/Yen	13.6
UK/Pound	11.9
Canadian Dollar	9.1
Swedish Krona	4.2
Swiss Franc	3.6

FIGURE 4.10 U.S. Dollar Index Against Gold Spot Price

FIGURE 4.11 USD/CHF and USD Index

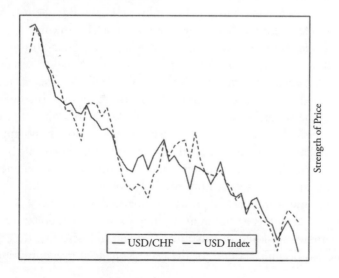

FIGURE 4.12   USD Index and ETF, UUP

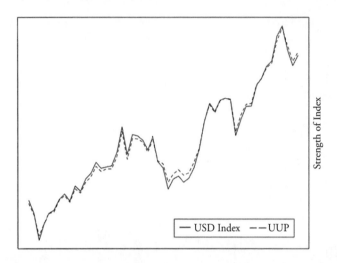

Fear of Deflation/Inflation

The dominant fundamental force relating to the dollar is fear. It's either fear of inflation or fear of a deflation reflected in a declining economy. It's surely complicated, particularly in the post-2008 financial collapse period that ushered in an era of very low rates and government increase of the money supply, known as quantitative easing. In November 2014, quantitative easing came to an end. The result may be, if the economy was stronger, expectations of increase in interest rates, and a dollar bullish climate. But the fear factor is real. There is fear of the U.S. government not being able to control its spending, and this leads to a weakness in the currency as confidence in the United States declines as a place for investments. This is not, however, certain, since problems elsewhere are often much worse. Generally, the macro force can be understood as: When the U.S. equity market is strong, the dollar loses its attractiveness—unless the U.S. equity market is so strong that interest rates are expected to go up! The converse situation is not always applicable. The U.S. dollar can at times be nearly 100 percent correlated with a positive direction in the S&P and at other times, just the opposite (Figure 4.13). When U.S. equity markets sell off, the U.S. dollar may also sell off—if the trigger event was fear of lack of growth or financial instability.

The general market weakness in recent years of the U.S. dollar is a specific case of currency weakness due to a fear of financial instability. Recently, the Eurozone has become a victim of the fear of financial instability, and often

FIGURE 4.13 U.S. Dollar and S&P Correlation Rate

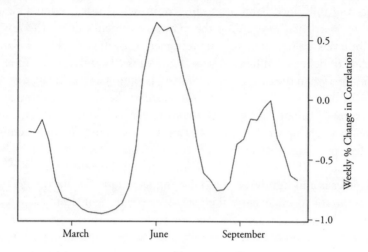

making the weak dollar a haven currency. This fear hit the EUR/USD over the problems of Greece, Spain, and Portugal. In the coming years, it is a near-certainty that the Eurozone will present the trader with many opportunities where fear of financial instability related to sovereign debt distorts price movements and increases volatility. It is therefore appropriate for the trader to understand sovereign debt as a force for underlying market movements and, in particular, currency moves (Figure 4.14).

FIGURE 4.14 Impacts of Increased Sovereign Debt on Currency Risk

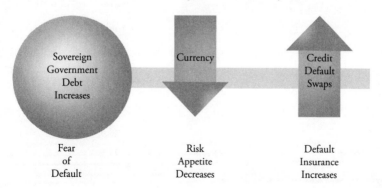

A theme to watch out for in trading binary options is news relating to deficits and unfunded liabilities facing countries. This fear often appears in the news, particularly regarding the U.S. government's debt. The fear that the debt levels are unsustainable often triggers a selloff in the U.S. dollar. The same fear of deficits and financial instability causes bearish sentiment regarding the euro when the debt problems facing Ireland, Greece, Spain, and so on appear in the news. It also causes an increase in the cost of insuring against a government default. We can see that a Greek two-year bond has interest payments much higher than the German two-year bond yield, reflecting the extra fear premium that the market imposed on Greece to make its bonds more attractive (Figure 4.15). While monitoring differences in government bond yields is a more advanced monitoring technique for the average trader, it is important to understand the fear of sovereign debt default is, and will continue to be, a major fundamental force.

This fear is not unfounded. Several countries are approaching huge financial burdens. It is often expressed as a percentage of the country's total Gross Domestic Product. The Organisation for Economic Co-operation and Development (OECD) tracks the key metrics of an economy (Table 4.2). We can see how different countries compare on this financial burden measure. Notice that the U.S. government deficit is now equal to what the United States produces in one year!

Traders should monitor this table!

TABLE 4.2 General Government Gross Financial Liabilities as a Percentage of GDP

	2010	2011	2014
Canada	84.4	85.5	107.6
France	92.4	97.1	119.2
Germany	79.9	81.3	82.2
Greece	129.2	136.8	179.8
Italy	131.3	132.7	156.2
Japan	198.4	204.2	231.9
Spain	72.2	78.2	97.7
Switzerland	42.1	41.1	34.7
United Kingdom	81.3	88.6	116.8
United States	92.8	98.5	123.2

Data source: OECD, www.oecd.org

FIGURE 4.15 Two-Year Bond Yields: Germany versus Greece

Notice that the United States's liabilities as a percentage of GDP has crossed the important psychological 100 percent level, thereby generating great attention.

Foreign Ownership of U.S. Treasuries

Another important sentiment indicator about the dollar is the amount and change in the holdings of U.S. Treasuries (Table 4.3) by foreign buyers. The U.S. Treasury International Capital System (TIC) report provides this information. China is the top owner of U.S. debt, purchasing $1.1 trillion of U.S. Treasuries! What would happen if China decided to slow down such purchases? The dollar would severely and negatively react. When rumors circulate that China may diversify away from such purchases, the U.S. dollar reacts with weakness. But it's important to realize that a precipitous decline in foreign purchases of U.S. debt is unlikely and would hurt those countries, such as China and Japan, which primarily also own almost $1 trillion worth of U.S. Treasuries. It's not only the amount they own, but whether the trend is up or down from the previous months or years.

An excellent index that tracks U.S. financial conditions is the Bloomberg U.S. Financial Conditions Index. The chart can be found at www.bloomberg .com/apps/quote?ticker=BFCIUS:IND.

Notice how the index plunged in September 2008 when the global financial collapse occurred (Figure 4.16). Also notice it recovered to near pre-collapse levels. This index, when it changes, provides important clues as to the larger financial economic U.S. conditions.

TABLE 4.3 Biggest Foreign Holders of U.S. Treasuries

Country	Holdings in March 2011	Holdings in January 2016
China	1.1 trillion	1.264 trillion
Japan	907 billion	1.144 trillion
United Kingdom	325 billion	214.1 billion
Oil Exporters	22.3 billion	289 billion
Brazil	193 billion	255 billion
Carib Banking	154 billion	337 billion
Switzerland	111 billion	227.1 billion

FIGURE 4.16 U.S. Financial Conditions Index

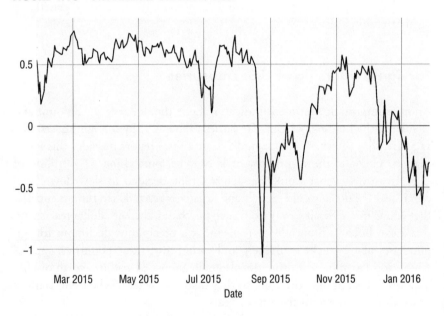

Crude Oil and the Historic Oil Price Plunge

Crude oil presents another major fundamental force in the world markets that binary option traders need to follow. Essentially, the demand for oil is based on global growth. If more growth is expected, more oil will be needed. Oil price valuation becomes a basic relationship between supply and demand. Surprise supplies dampen the price, and surprise shortages increase the price. Oil prices also can increase when there is a global crisis, particularly a crisis centered in the Middle East, since that region produces the majority of the world's oil supplies.

Note: Binary oil options are *not* on the more popular Brent crude oil contract, but it is on the West Texas Intermediate (WTI). However, they move very closely, but not perfectly, together (Figure 4.17). It is also noteworthy about the relationship between oil prices and the U.S. dollar. A strong dollar results in lower oil prices. Also, when oil prices fall back, the effect is a stimulus in exports. High oil prices result in a weaker dollar as the U.S. trade deficit increases. This lowers the GDP. The relationship between the U.S. dollar and crude oil prices overall is a negative co-movement (Figure 4.18). A very acceptable way of trading oil in the binary market is to trade the USD/CAD cross pair because Canada is an oil exporter (tar sands oil) and when oil prices increase, the Canadian dollar tends to strengthen against the U.S. dollar. But note that this is only opposite because of the currency pair being the USD/CAD. If the chart is CAD/USD, the co-movements of oil and the Canadian dollar would be in the same direction (Figure 4.19).

The historic selloff in oil during 2015 offers a good example of the power of binary option out-of-the-money trading strategies. The strategies that best apply to big selloffs are breakout binary plays and deep-out-of-the-money plays. This points to a mixed strategy in which a portion of the trades put on are always deep-out-of-the-money plays mixed with ATM and in-the-money plays. When a big move happens, the deep-out-of-the-money plays will catch the moves. Keep in mind when a big bullish move happens, buying a deep-in-the-money position goes with the crowd. If a selloff occurs, betting that it won't go back up by selling a deep-in-the-money resistance leg is an appropriate strategy.

FIGURE 4.17 Brent Crude Oil and WTI

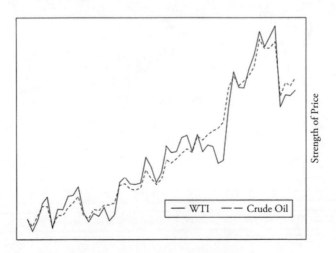

FIGURE 4.18   Crude and U.S. Dollar Index

FIGURE 4.19   Crude Oil Plunge

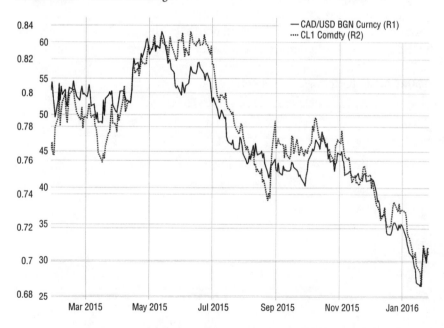

The EUR/USD for Binary Trading

The Eurozone was feared to collapse because of the Greek debt crises. It survived it, but the Euro itself has been in a bearish trend since reaching on April 20, 2014, the high of 1.3867 (Figure 4.20). This is mainly due to the lack of inflation in the Eurozone. The European Central Bank under Draghi has a goal of stimulating the Eurozone and therefore has had a policy of monetary expansion. This is in great contrast to the end of monetary expansion in the United States. The binary trader of the EUR/USD needs to not only carefully assess the price patterns in the euro, but be very diligent relating to economic reports on eurozone inflation. These reports are likely to move the EUR/USD. The binary trader should be watching when the ECB issues its interest rate and monetary policy reports. In the coming years, the weakness in the EUR/USD points to the potential for the EUR/USD to have parity with the U.S. dollar.

Carry Trade and Interest Rate Differentials

At this point we have reviewed specific powerful global fundamental forces that help traders understand what moves markets. In recent years, global interest rates remained at historic low levels in order to stimulate growth

FIGURE 4.20 Monthly EUR/USD Chart

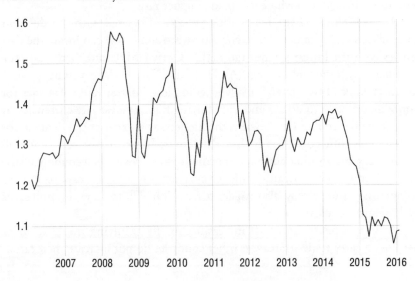

after the financial collapse in September 2008. However, interest rates have begun to increase at least in the United States, and this might be ushering in a period of tightening of monetary policy, and tightening rates. The result is the return (it never really left) of one of the most important forces that move currencies: interest rate differentials. These can be considered the jet stream of the currency market! Any binary option trader looking to trade the currency pairs offered by Nadex (USD/JPY, USD/CAD, USD/CHF, EUR/USD, EUR/JPY, GBP/JPY, AUD/UST, GPB/USD) must understand how interest rate differentials and expectations move price action. We could write a book about this subject alone. Namely, interest rates and interest rate differences are prime forces that move the currency pairs (Table 4.4). Another way to view the interest rate force is to see it as a global jet stream of the money flows.

Here is how it works. In a very basic way, currencies will strengthen if the interest rates of the economy are expected to increase in value. They will weaken if the interest rates are expected to decline. Central banks have the role through monetary policy to adjust interest rates to control and minimize inflation. Higher rates discourage economic activity and are used as a throttle when an economy is perceived to be growing too fast.

But that is only part of the story. In currency trading, the value of one currency is always assessed against the value of another currency. That is why they are called currency pairs. For example, the EUR/USD is a currency pair in which the euro is traded against the U.S. dollar. For this pair, when the European Central Bank increases interest rates, and the United States does not, the net effect is bullish for the euro against the dollar, because money will tend to be attracted to where it is paid a higher rate.

A quick check of the major interest rates associated with the different currencies reveals dramatic differences between some. We can locate the currencies with the lowest interest rates (JPY, CHF, USD), and then locate the currencies with the highest rates (AUD, NZD). This leads to a strategy called the *carry trade*. This strategy involves selling low interest rate currencies (or borrowing money to do so) and then buying high interest rate currencies. It is no coincidence that the Aussie is the highest, as it experienced demand for its resources. But going too high is dangerous. If a currency gets very high in value against another currency, it actually slows down the economy of the high priced currency because a higher currency value means exports are less competitive. But it may also trigger a recession. Ultimately, the process is cyclical and self-correcting.

As U.S. interest rates start increasing, in effect, buying the U.S. dollar becomes a carry trade strategy, as other countries do not increase their rates.

Central Bankers Move the Markets

The binary option trader needs to track impending central bank decisions and statements. Their words are powerful triggers for market sentiment to cascade through the social media. By closely following central bank statements and minutes, the trader will get, in advance, one of the best leading indicators for whether conditions are suitable for different trading strategies. When a central bank statement is due, consider an out-of-the-money strategy. It is more appropriate than a deep-in-the-money strategy, because there is a high potential for a surprise in the statement.

Checklist for Currency Pairs

Trading binary options in currency pairs provides a virtual round-the-clock opportunity from the opening of the Asian session on Monday morning until the close of the New York session. Depending on the firm, actual opening and closing times for trading may vary.

There are several items that the trader should know about in evaluating market conditions relating to the currency pairs. A key feature is that currency prices are not random and reflect major economic forces and sentiment expectations. The following are some of the terms to study and know in order to evaluate currency pairs.

- *Interest rate expectations:* Interest rate expectations are the key drivers of currency-pair price action. When interest rates are expected to rise, the currency pair will become more attractive and therefore attract demand. The general effect is the pair increases in value.
- *Relative growth:* If one country is growing faster than another, the currency of the stronger growth country will tend to be stronger as it attracts capital.
- *Data releases:* Currency pairs are extremely sensitive to economic data releases. Disappointing GDP results in a weakening of the currency. Surprise positive data generally increases the value of the currency.
- *Resistance and support:* These daily and weekly levels are important for currencies as $5 trillion a day is exchanged; intraday movements are subject to noise trading and not that meaningful.
- *Commodity-based currency pairs:* The USD/CAD and the AUD/USD, are the main commodity-based pairs and move in reaction to commodity markets.

- *Cross pairs:* These exclude the U.S. dollar. Binary options on GBP/JPY and EUR/JPY are available. Cross pairs exhibit more predictable patterns because the U.S. dollar is excluded and this removes a lot of potential noise.

Bitcoin as a Binary

Bitcoin has emerged as a new underlying market for binary traders. It is now being offered on the Nadex and IG market platforms. Also, many OTC firms offer Bitcoin binaries. There are two important points that the binary trader should have in mind when trading Bitcoin binaries. First, Bitcoin has great volatility. Sudden movement happens without clues leading up to those movements. The result is that out-of-the money buy or sell trades make the most sense. Second, Bitcoin actual prices are not transparent. At Nadex, a new index called TeraBitcoin Index is used to provide the quote stream at Nadex. At IG, Bitcoin (XBT/USD) quotes are a composite of the price of Bitcoin from several Bitcoin exchanges.

But at other binary firms, which offer Bitcoin high-low binaries, it is not at all transparent which Bitcoin exchange is used. For those who trade Bitcoin binaries, there is, however, a major advantage: Bitcoin prices are the least correlated with the other underlying markets and this in theory reduces the total volatility of a return of the total portfolio of the trader.

Using an Economic Calendar as Trading Tool

The economic data calendar should be thought of as a key fundamental analysis and binary option trading tool. Many sites offer economic calendars and they are easy to access. *It is so important that no one should trade without the calendar being reviewed first.* Not knowing that an economic data release is scheduled to appear leaves your binary option trade subject to great risk. The economic calendar provides a critical and advanced alert function for the binary option trader. It lists the time of economic data releases. These releases provide key measures relating to economic performance in countries around the world. The markets pay close attention to these releases and react to any surprises in them. In weeks in which key economic data releases will occur, there is certain to be greater volatility.

The binary option trader has two basic approaches relating to trading the economic data releases. The first approach is to view economic data releases as a factor in raising the overall volatility level of the markets during that week.

Greater volatility benefits strategies that choose deeper-out-of-the-money strike prices because of the tendency of prices to move with greater momentum in reaction to surprise announcements. But a cautionary note is in order regarding volatility. It is not simply the level of volatility that is important, but its rate of change. When volatility is at extremes, it can be a reversal signal. Traders view high volatility as a sell signal and low volatility as a buy signal. How to track volatility will be reviewed in a later chapter.

Alternatively, the trader can view a particular economic data release as a directly tradable event. In this context, the trader can anticipate a bullish or bearish direction, and choose a corresponding strike price. However, what happens if the trader wants to trade a big surprise, but doesn't know which way the market will react? He can, in fact, use binary option trading to play a breakout in either direction. This is similar to a straddle strategy in regular options. A third approach is to wait for the economic release to occur and develop a trading strategy after the market reaction to the news.

Look Online

These websites have proven to be useful in providing basic information and tools that binary option traders can use to identify forces affecting the markets, track their trades, and improve their results.

www.forexfactory.com

www.chinaview.cn

http://adv.org

www.chinamoney.com.cn

www.treasury.gov/resource-center/data-chart-center/tic/Documents/mfh.txt

www.bis.org/cbanks.htm

www.ino.com

www.rexpros.com

CHAPTER 5

Basic Technical Analysis

This chapter reviews basic technical analysis that will help shape binary option trading. If you are a beginning trader, going through the key technical analysis steps will help you develop core skills that can be applied in any market. Binary option trading is an ideal place for a new trader and this chapter provides a review of basic technical analysis concepts and techniques that will help improve the skill level of the binary option trader. The more experienced trader can use it as a quick review or skip these sections.

Confirming fundamental conditions through technical indicators is a key phase for preparing to trade binary options. Beginning traders have a tendency to anchor their trades on one indicator or type of information. But making a trading decision is multi-dimensional. It is really about pattern recognition. Ask yourself what pattern the underlying market is in. Is the underlying market trending up, down, or sideways? Is the price experiencing an increasing momentum? Is it at extremes? Is volatility low or high? Is it testing support or resistance? These and other questions come quickly to the mind of the trader who needs to effectively prepare for trading binary options. They become, in effect, a checklist of technical conditions that need to be reviewed. Let's look at candlesticks, trend lines, and support and resistance lines. These three categories create a solid foundation for trading, and apply very effectively to binary option trading decisions.

Key Candlestick Patterns

If you are new to trading, you need to become familiar with *candlesticks*. Candlesticks are a common way to represent price activity. They originated with the Japanese when they were trading rice hundreds of years ago. Today,

FIGURE 5.1   Key Parts of Candlesticks

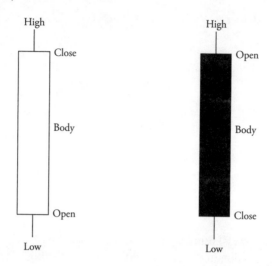

candlestick patterns are the most popular way to represent price activity. Let's start with understanding the basic structure of candles (Figure 5.1).

Each candle has four parts. *Wicks* represent the lowest and highest points reached. There is the *body*, which has a top and bottom representing the open and close prices. These four components are, in effect, the DNA of price action. Any emotion in the market is ultimately represented in the candlestick pattern.

A candle can represent price activity for almost any desired time frame. There can be one-minute, five-minute, one-hour, one-day, one-week, and one-month candles. When a trader selects a time period, the candle represents that time frame. For example, 50 candles on a 5-minute time period represents 50 × 5 minutes, or 250 minutes of price activity.

One of the most important and basic features of the candlestick is its color. It is conventional to have a white candle representing a bullish activity and a black candle representing a bearish activity. Many charts allow traders to use their own colors to represent being bullish or bearish. Let's look at what being bullish or bearish really mean in the context of what the candlestick is doing.

A bullish candle is one in which the close price is above the opening price. A bearish candle is one in which the close price is below the opening. Basically, the direction is either north or south! There are times when the open and close are the same or nearly the same. The candles are then neither bullish nor bearish. This represents indecision or hesitation. Candles are all about expressing the emotion in the market. They are, in fact, emotional landmarks. It is commonplace to look at the market as a battle between buyers and sellers. If this is so, then the candlesticks are snapshots in time of who is winning that battle. All the patterns of the market that are possible are really single candles grouped together representing the price activity as it moves in time. There are many candle patterns; following are some of the most important ones: *Hammer* (Figure 5.2), *Doji* (Figure 5.3), *Spinning Tops* (Figure 5.4), *Engulfing Candles* (Figure 5.5), and *Tweezers* (Figure 5.6).

It's a good idea to study these patterns and try to get familiar with them in the context of market action. They will confirm the emotional status of the market. Hammer patterns are called that because they look like a hammer. It is characterized by having a long wick, sometimes twice the body size. When a hammer appears, it is usually a reversal sign. Dojis are very important in showing hesitation and indecision. There is virtually no body since the open and close price points turn out to be nearly the same. Spinning tops are related to market indecision as well since they have small bodies. The engulfing candle is considered a very good indicator of a change in the mood of the market. It is a pattern of a small candle followed by a very big body of an opposite color. That is why it is called engulfing. Tweezer candles demonstrate strong support or resistance. When a tweezer is at the bottom, the bears have failed to push the price lower. When tweezer formations are at the top of a candle, it signifies a failure to push the price higher. It is important to keep in mind that the predictability of the emotion signified by a candlestick is related to the time frame. One-minute candles are not as predictive as one-hour candles. In binary option trading, four-hour and one-day candles provide a good source of reliable emotional information about the market.

FIGURE 5.2 Hammer—Bullish

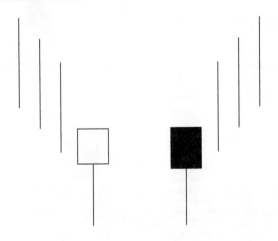

FIGURE 5.3 Dojis

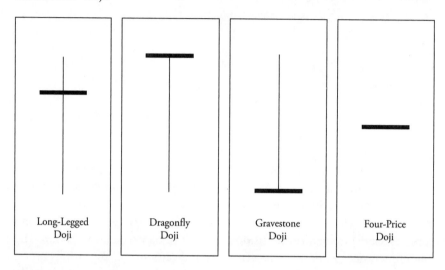

| Long-Legged | Dragonfly | Gravestone | Four-Price |
| Doji | Doji | Doji | Doji |

FIGURE 5.4 Doji Followed by Reversal

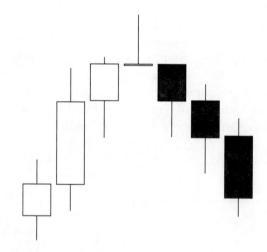

FIGURE 5.5 Spinning Tops—Indecision

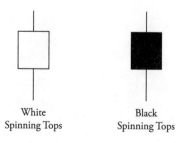

White
Spinning Tops

Black
Spinning Tops

FIGURE 5.6 Engulfing Candles

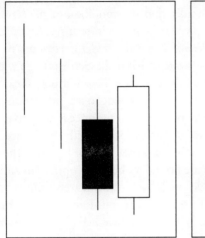 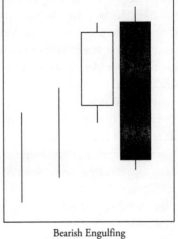

Bullish Engulfing   Bearish Engulfing

FIGURE 5.7 Tweezers

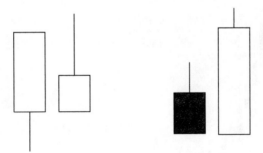

Trend Lines

Trend lines are one of the basic tools for trading in all markets. But even though trend lines are basic, they remain one of the most important and effective tools a binary option trader can use. The trader who learns how to use trend lines for shaping a diagnosis of the market patterns is likely to rely a lot less on the many technical indicators that are commonly used. Let's explore trend lines further. First, let's define our terms. There are two types of trends: an uptrend and a downtrend.

An *uptrend* is a situation in which the prices keep getting higher highs and also higher lows. A *downtrend* occurs when there are lower highs and lower lows. Trend lines help the binary option trader find the condition of the sentiment in the market. In fact, we can restate what a trend is in terms of sentiment. *It can be viewed as a persistence of sentiment.* When the trader determines that the sentiment is strong, the binary option strategy that makes sense is to go with the sentiment. If the trader determines that the sentiment is very strong, the choices are more difficult. A very strong trend may be a prelude to a continuation of the action; however, it may also be a contra-indicator that the price is ready to reverse.

We can see that the power of trend analysis is its ability to project into the future. Trend lines are not indicators, and they are not lagging. They are, in fact, sentiment maps that define the boundary between optimism and fear.

Many beginning traders don't know how to draw a trend line and as a result misjudge the price action. To ensure that you know how to draw a trend line correctly, let's review the key steps involved. First, we present the steps in drawing a downtrend line (Figure 5.8). Second, we present the steps in drawing an uptrend line (Figure 5.9).

FIGURE 5.8   Drawing a Downtrend Line

Find the highest high, then connect to the next lower high and extend.

FIGURE 5.9 Drawing an Uptrend Line

Find the lowest low,
then the next higher low
and extend out.

The steps for drawing a downtrend line are:

1. Locate the recent high.
2. Draw a line next to the immediate lower high.
3. Extend the line to the right end of the chart beyond the latest date into the future.

The steps for drawing an uptrend line are:

1. Find lowest low.
2. Find the next higher low following the lowest low.
3. Draw a line from the lowest low to the higher low and extend it into the future.

The trend lines need to only connect the candlestick lows or highs and not the candle bodies. Figure 5.10 shows an incorrect drawing of the lines.

Beyond understanding how to draw trend lines, the trader needs to be able to detect whether there is an outer and an inner trend. The presence of an inner trend line indicates a shift in sentiment and momentum and should

FIGURE 5.10   Incorrectly Drawn Trend Line

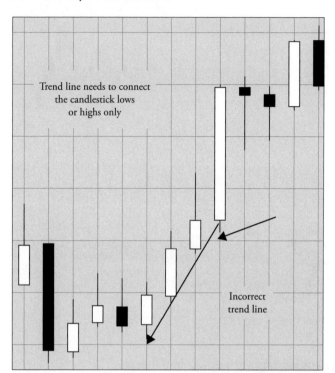

be an alert that conditions are changing fast. The trader can also use the outer trend line as a boundary where the price will have difficulty in breaking. So finding an outer and inner trend line helps locate the right binary option strike price (Figure 5.11).

A useful exercise is to profile the trend conditions. Try to answer the questions: Is the price above or below the day trend line in the intended direction of the trade? Is the 50-day moving average in agreement with the trend direction? Is the 21-day moving average above or below the 50-day moving average? (See Figure 5.12.)

Support and Resistance

A foundation for all of trading is being able to describe what the price activity is doing on a chart. Reading the chart is a process of identifying and describing where the price is and what it is doing. A basic tool is resistance

FIGURE 5.11 Outer and Inner Trend Lines

Inner Trend Lines

Outer Trend Line

and support lines (Figure 5.13). They provide evidence where the emotions of the market are clustered. Let's define some key terms and illustrate it in a chart.

Support is where the price stops falling and comes to a temporary rest. This area is called support. It is as if the price stopped falling and is resting on a floor. *Resistance* is the point at which the price stops rising and comes to a pause. It is as if a ceiling has formed.

The first step in drawing a resistance or support line is to locate the price action on the chart (Figure 5.14). In reviewing the price movement, try to answer the questions: Where is the most recent low? Where is the most recent high? Then draw a horizontal line under the low and then above the high. Support and resistance do not form instantly. Confirmation is usually needed to be sure that there is a zone of support. This often means waiting to see three failed attempts to break support or resistance.

FIGURE 5.12 Trend Conditions Checklist

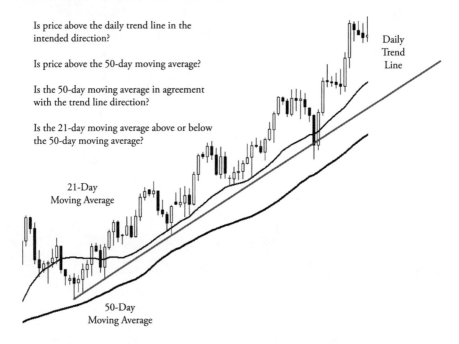

Is price above the daily trend line in the
intended direction?

Is price above the 50-day moving average?

Is the 50-day moving average in agreement
with the trend line direction?

Is the 21-day moving average above or below
the 50-day moving average?

21-Day
Moving Average

Daily
Trend
Line

50-Day
Moving Average

FIGURE 5.13 Basic Support and Resistance Lines

Resistance

Support

FIGURE 5.14 How Support and Resistance Lines Form

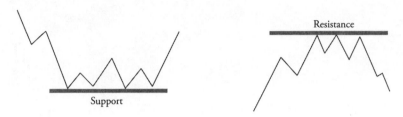

Finding support and resistance is one of the first steps in developing a trading strategy. If a trader wants to buy into the market, one of the best locations to buy will be near a support area. If a trader wants to sell into the market, one of the best locations to sell will be near a resistance area. This is because if there is strong support, it is likely that a low in the price has been established and if there is strong resistance, it is likely that a high in the price has been established. Trading near support and resistance helps achieve the goal of buying low and selling high. In short, once a support line or resistance line is established, it has identified for you a top and a bottom. Locating a support and resistance line is also important because it will help reduce the risk of loss of a trade.

Another feature of support and resistance lines is what happens when a price goes through a support line and falls below it. What happens when a price goes through a resistance line and pushes above it? When these events occur, and they occur all the time, the support line begins to act as a new resistance line. The resistance line begins to act as a new support line (Figure 5.15). We can see this shift and intimate relationship between support and resistance in Figure 5.16.

An important question that should be asked is this: How strong is the support or resistance? The stronger the support or resistance lines, the greater the confidence the trader has in using these lines to shape a trade. There are many ways of identifying the degree of weakness or strength of support and

FIGURE 5.15 Resistance Becomes Support

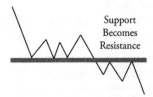

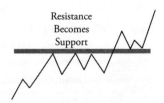

FIGURE 5.16 Support Transforms to Resistance

resistance lines. The first tool is the price itself. If a support or resistance line has been touched many times, this indicates that the line is strong and holding the price from going through it. Many traders use three touches to confirm that the lines are good lines to locate possible entry positions. It's useful to keep in mind that higher time frames provide more evidence of the strength of support or resistance. When a price action is probing a day support or resistance line, it is evidence that sentiment is changing much more than a price action probing an hourly support or resistance line. This logic further confirms that four-hour, day, and one-week price action charts should be the basis for trading weekly binary option contracts.

As you can see, support and resistance is not one-dimensional. Making a judgment about the strength of support and resistance requires a multiple time analysis as well as looking at the price action in relationship to other patterns such as Bollinger Bands and the presence or absence of doji candles (Figure 5.17).

FIGURE 5.17 Support and Resistance Checklist

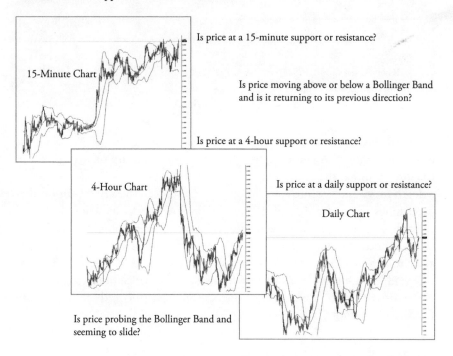

Is price at a 15-minute support or resistance?

15-Minute Chart

Is price moving above or below a Bollinger Band and is it returning to its previous direction?

Is price at a 4-hour support or resistance?

4-Hour Chart

Is price at a daily support or resistance?

Daily Chart

Is price probing the Bollinger Band and seeming to slide?

Confirming Strength with Price Break Charts

Because detecting direction in the underlying market is so important, the trader should look to confirm the decisions and conclusions made using the basic trend line, candlestick, resistance, and support tools. A very powerful chart tool and technique to use is price breaks. The book *Sentiment Indicators* provides a very detailed view of price break charts for the very serious trader, but this chapter provides a basic understanding necessary for applying it to binary option trading.

Price break charts have their origins with Japanese traders. There was little Western awareness of them until the publication of Steve Nison's book, *Beyond Candlesticks: New Japanese Charting Techniques Revealed* (Nison 1994). In effect, this book reintroduced price break charts to the United States. Price break charts provide a powerful ability to detect the strength of a trend and where it will end. As a result, they can be a very effective tool for binary option trading. Let's first look at the basics of price break charts.

TIP

Price break charts are available for free access by downloading the following platform:

    http://downloads.solotrader.com/WorldTradingTeam/World TradingTeamSoloTrader.exe.

Price break charts look like candlesticks without the wicks. They are bricks or columns. A good way to view them is as steps up or steps down in the direction that the sentiment is taking. They usually have a black color for a down move and a white color for an upward move. The key condition that determines the generation of a black brick is whether a new low has been created. If a new low has been created, a new black column is added or painted onto the chart. If a new high has been reached, then a new white column appears (Figure 5.18). If no new low or high has been achieved, nothing is added. One of the most beneficial aspects of price break charts is the clarity of their rules. Because they operate on close prices, there is no room for dispute (Figure 5.19).

FIGURE 5.18 Three-Line Break Chart Showing Bullish Reversal

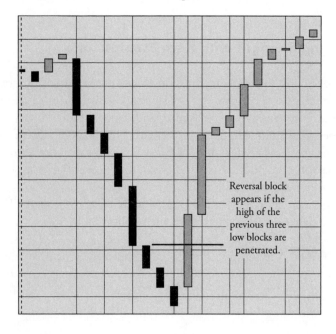

Reversal block appears if the high of the previous three low blocks are penetrated.

FIGURE 5.19   Three-Line Break Chart Showing Bearish Reversal

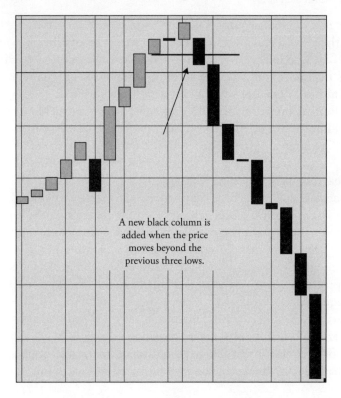

A new black column is added when the price moves beyond the previous three lows.

Price break charts may seem simplistic because they result from a simple set of rules, but they unleash a great deal of technical analysis. From the perspective of sentiment analysis, by registering only the occurrences when a price is establishing a new high or a new low, the chart is in effect visualizing the persistence of sentiment. The price's ability to persist in setting new highs or new lows provides a way to quantify trends other than by using traditional trend analysis. It goes beyond the simple criterion of having higher highs and higher lows, or lower highs and lower lows. When we say a trend is in place, don't we mean that there is a persistence of sentiment? Viewing it from the perspective of persistence, the trader can begin to quantify how serious a trend is, when it is weakening, and when it has reversed. Price break charts measure this persistence in an unambiguous way. Using price break charts, the trader cannot dispute the facts of the price action; either the price has succeeded in persisting higher or lower, or it has not. The trader also knows in advance where a price break chart would be considered strong enough to break the trend.

Pattern of Block Sequences

The presence of block sequences is a key visual clue. If there is a long series of blocks, the trend direction is strong but can in fact be entering an end phase. A good idea is to look for very small sized blocks. This shows hesitation and presents the trader with a clue to an impending breakout (Figure 5.20). The trader's task is to evaluate when a long series is in fact in its end stage. There is no definitive, preset rule regarding how many consecutive blocks represent an entry into an overextended area. Block sequences will vary by instrument and by time interval. A good idea is for the trader to scan the sequences that have appeared over the previous week and determine how many consecutive blocks have actually appeared. This approach ensures that the sentiment of the immediate environment is captured, rather than a predefined view that eight or 10 consecutive blocks represent a series that is about to end. If, for example, a trader using a five-minute price break chart determines that there have not been more than 21 consecutive black or white blocks, the trader can assume that if a series is in place that is approaching 21 blocks, there is a high probability that a reversal is about to occur. This kind of perusal of block sequences works very well. A more precise quantification is not difficult to achieve for the diligent, more mathematically inclined trader. In fact, one can generate a bell curve or standard deviation analysis of block sequences. It is also not an accident that Fibonacci resistance lines, when applied to price break chart blocks, often coincide with projected reversal points.

FIGURE 5.20 Small Block Reveals Tired Trend

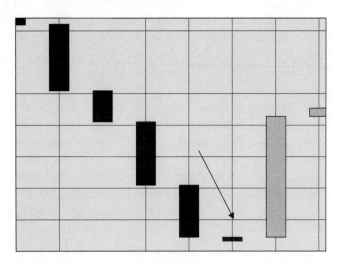

We need to state strongly that price break charts do not predict the coming of a reversal. They do tell us where such a reversal would be considered significant. Price break charts actually and precisely define and project where, not when, such a price reversal will appear. By definition, a reversal block will appear if the price gives back or retraces a given number of previous highs or lows! The trader knows in advance where a reversal will be powerful enough to generate a confirming new reversal color.

Is a Reversal Serious?

Very often, the binary option trader will confront a reversal in price direction in the candlestick chart. To determine the best strategy in the context of this kind of reversal, the question that needs to be answered is: Is it serious? This is where three-line break charts really help. A three-line break chart will very often not show a reversal, while a candlestick chart does. When this happens, the trader needs to question the conclusion that a reversal has occurred. Reversals can be short-lived, especially if they are occurring on an intraday time frame. A three-line break reversal, once detected, is not necessarily permanent. The trader should wait for another new high or low to feel more confident. It's important to answer the questions:

- Is the reversal near a Fibonacci resistance line?
- Is the reversal in the direction of the larger trend?
- Is the reversal consistent with the existing ratio of the number of consecutive highs to lows?

Figure 5.21 shows a scenario in which the price reversed right at a 61.8 percent Fibonacci resistance line. This is an ideal condition!

Getting familiar with three-line break charts will benefit the binary option trader because it will provide an unambiguous tool for evaluating the trend conditions in the market. By using three-line break charts, the trader will accomplish four important analytical objectives:

1. Determine the strength of the trend in place.
2. Determine whether the trend is tiring.
3. Determine if a reversal has occurred and whether it is serious.
4. Select binary option strike prices.

Traders can learn more about the three-line break at www.learn4x .com/3Line.

FIGURE 5.21   Three-Line Break Charts and Fibonacci

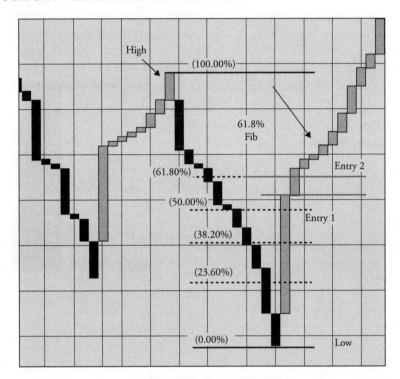

Examples of Three-Line Break Charts for Underlying Markets

Let's look at examples using price break with an underlying market and apply the analysis to illustrate the kind of thinking a binary option trade involves. A trader looking at the AUD/USD three-line break chart (Figure 5.22) sees that the Aussie had a sequence of consecutive new-day highs, followed by a reversal of two consecutive new lows, and then followed by another reversal up. The trader could, looking at this pattern conclude that the pattern is very weak bullish. Any weak news on global growth could cause a reversal and the binary option strike price below the previous low would be a target.

Let's look at oil. The West Texas oil three-line break chart (Figure 5.23) shows the dramatic reversal of oil prices in February 2011 was followed by seven consecutive new-day highs. Then came a big reversal down. This was followed by a reversal up. When a reversal is followed by another reversal, it is a very strong signal that the resumption of the direction is strong. At the end of the chart is a big reversal down, followed by a smaller new-day low, followed by a much smaller new-day low. This is showing that bearish sentiment in oil was still there but getting tired.

FIGURE 5.22   AUD/USD Three-Line Break Chart

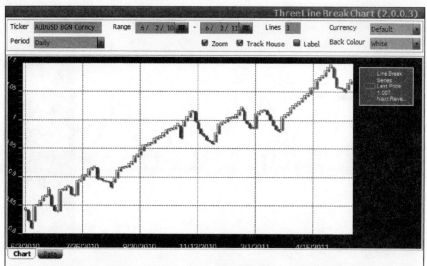

FIGURE 5.23   West Texas Crude Three-Line Break Chart

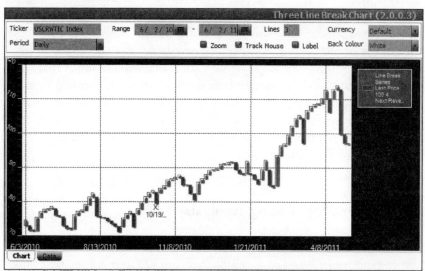

FIGURE 5.24   GBP/JPY Three-Line Break Chart

GPLB GBPJPY   CurncyGPLB

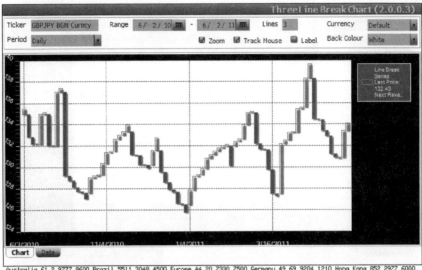

Australia 61 2 9777 8600 Brazil 5511 3048 4500 Europe 44 20 7330 7500 Germany 49 69 9204 1210 Hong Kong 852 2977 6000
Japan 81 3 3201 8900   Singapore 65 6212 1000   U.S. 1 212 318 2000   Copyright 2011 Bloomberg Finance L.P.
                                                    SN 730339 EDT GMT-4:00 H201-1470-0 02-Jun-2011 21:06:17

The binary option trader seeing this chart could justify an at-the-money binary option contract at 100. This would play a bounce back.

The GBP/JPY cross pair represents a very good example of a wave pattern detected by the three-line break chart (Figure 5.24). This pair shows a sequence of alternating sequences of new highs and then back to lows. It is a great example of the power of a three-line break. Notice that when a reversal occurs, it's very rare to have the reversal brick followed immediately by another reversal. This provides an excellent clue as to where to locate the binary option strike price that offers maximum support or resistance. A buyer would locate the strike price that is below the point of the most recent upward break at 130.00.

Key Patterns for Trading Analysis

We are not yet done with basic technical analysis. Trend analysis, and support and resistance analysis, is an excellent foundation. However, the next building block to establish stronger trading skills is to understand the key patterns.

FIGURE 5.25 USD/JPY Three-Line Break Chart

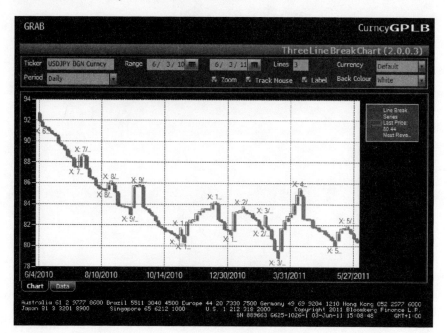

Once the underlying market is chosen, it's time to conduct a pattern analysis. The first choice is the time interval for the charts. The four-hour time interval represents an effective middle ground. One can gain a sense of the big picture, as well as of the near-term changes in sentiment. For those trading intra-day, the 30-minute time frame can be used.

While there are many patterns that are formed by price action, the ones that all traders should know are the *triangle, channel, parabolic,* and *Bollinger Bands.* Let's look at some examples.

Triangles

Notice the formation of the triangle: price action starting at a wide range between the low and high and developing incrementally smaller ranges leading to almost no difference between the low and high. The market is telling the trader that a breakout is about to happen. Triangles come in a variety of forms (Figure 5.26). There are ascending triangles, descending triangles, and equilateral triangles. Triangles are classic visualizations of a cluster of sentiment. The triangle is a compression of the range between highs and lows.

FIGURE 5.26   Symmetrical, Descending, and Ascending Triangles

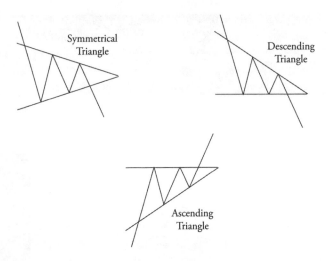

This means the battle between bullish and bearish sentiment is coming to a breakout point. Triangles can be considered preludes to breakouts. The binary option trader, when seeing a triangle, should locate the strike prices outside of the triangle and play a breakout. This is usually an out-of-the-money strategy. It can also be a deep-out-of-the-money strategy.

The triangle can be considered a barometer of emotions and indicates that the buyers and the sellers are lacking enough energy to dominate each other. The distance between the highs and the lows in the triangle are getting smaller until it goes to an apex, or point. When the trader sees a triangle, it means that there is likely to be a breakout.

The challenge for the trader is to recognize that there is a triangle forming and then prepare to trade. The trader prepares to trade the triangles with a breakout trade. An ascending triangle is likely to break out to the upside and resume its trend direction that was up. A descending triangle is likely to break out to the downside and then resume its trend direction, which was down. Lastly, a symmetrical triangle is likely to break out in either direction.

Hesitation or Consolidation Patterns: The Triangle and the Doji

Often in viewing price movements, it looks like prices move chaotically. But closer monitoring of price movements will often reveal patterns. One of the most important kinds of patterns is seen after a big move. After a big move, which is perhaps a response to news, the market goes into a period where it's digesting new information and is hesitating. Hesitation means that it is ranging, but it also means that the market is preparing to make a decision. You know this by noticing that the range is getting narrower. The difference between the highs and lows becomes smaller because the buyers and sellers are giving up and have no strong sentiment to keep the range that has existed. Hesitation is a prelude to a shift to a new direction or a confirmation that the prior direction before the hesitation should be resumed. Several hesitation patterns have become useful in trading. You can trade on the bounce of the price, or you can wait for a break but wait further for the price to come back into the sideways channel. This would provide confirmation that the pattern is still in force.

The most famous set of hesitation patterns is this class of doji candles (Figure 5.27). These candles reflect the emotional status of indecision. The opening and closing of a price is exactly the same. If during any period of

FIGURE 5.27   Doji Candle Types

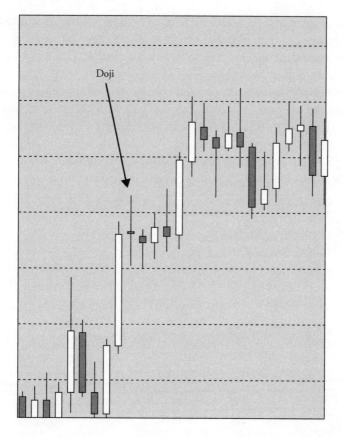

FIGURE 5.28   Doji Shows Hesitation

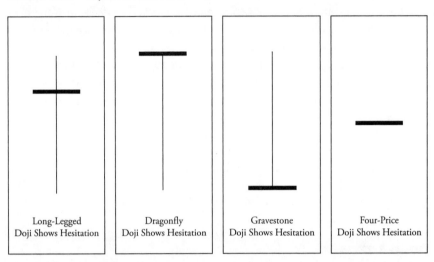

| Long-Legged
Doji Shows Hesitation | Dragonfly
Doji Shows Hesitation | Gravestone
Doji Shows Hesitation | Four-Price
Doji Shows Hesitation |

time the opening and closing is the same, it means the buyers and sellers are in equilibrium and therefore the sentiment is hesitating. When a doji appears, it doesn't necessarily mean a reversal is coming (Figure 5.28). But what happens after the doji is important.

Channels are the signature of stability and consistency. Their wave-like visuals underscore the predictive cycle, like oscillations of price swings from highs to lows (Figure 5.29). When detecting a channel, the trader is detecting the fact that the market sentiment is continuing. The trader therefore should go with the trend, and in-the-money strategies work with these conditions. Seeing a channel pattern is a welcome event for traders because it provides multiple opportunities

FIGURE 5.29   Channels

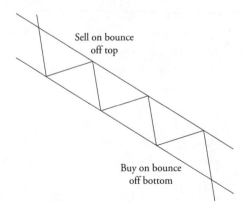

Sell on bounce
off top

Buy on bounce
off bottom

FIGURE 5.30 Parabolic Pattern

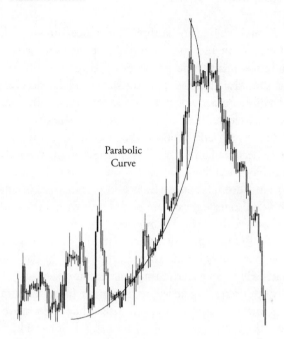

Parabolic
Curve

to trade. Traders can trade in either direction as long as the price is bouncing off the sides. We see in the following chart a representation of a downward channel. Notice that the bounce points are in both directions. This is what makes a channel important. It allows a trader more opportunity to trade in either direction.

The *parabolic pattern* is a reflection of strong momentum and is powered by crowd mania, particularly when it is forming an apex (Figure 5.30). This is a reversal signal. However, if the parabolic is in its early stages, joining the crowd with ATM strategies would be a ride on the momentum.

This pattern is called a parabolic because it actually follows the shape of a curved path known as a parabolic path. What is most important about it is that once a trader sees this pattern, it is a very strong indicator that the price is at an extreme. The parabolic pattern occurs because there is a rush of buying or selling. This rush of buying or selling shows crowd behavior. It starts because traders see an opportunity to make a profit, and other traders watching this start buy because they fear they will miss the opportunity. The emotion is self-fulfilling until the shape of the candles reaches an angle of nearly 90 degrees. This kind of shape cannot last long and it shows the sentiment is at its maximum. When a trader sees a parabolic pattern, it is a leading indicator that the price move will end, pause, and often reverse. This pattern appears in all time frames.

Fibonacci Resistance Lines

In her book *Fibonacci Analysis,* author Constance Brown said, "To understand market expansion and contraction, you need to understand the difference between ratios, means, and proportion," (Brown 2008, 16).

The trader should at all times apply the standard Fibonacci resistance tool to the price action of the underlying market. Fibonacci ratios are a key pattern and apply to all price patterns. These ratios have been the subject of many books and studies. No experienced trader ignores Fibonacci lines. If you don't know them, it's important to become familiar with their application. We really don't know why traders use Fibonacci lines, but part of the reason is that it is a self-fulfilling prophecy. As traders deem Fibonacci lines as important, they become important. Stops and limits and puts and calls are placed near them. They essentially work because traders believe they work. *In any case, Fibonacci lines do not predict where the market will be.* But they provide powerful markers as to where resistance and support will be. For binary option trading, the weekly or daily, and four-hour time price charts will be an effective time frame to use.

For binary option trading decisions, Fibonacci lines are an important tool. When markets move in response to event risks, they often move in Fibonacci ratios. Here are the three steps involved for using Fibonacci lines with binary option trading:

1. Locate on the weekly or daily chart the appropriate Fibonacci line.
2. After applying the Fibonacci line, determine where the price is in relationship to the key Fibonacci ratios.
3. Once you choose the binary option strike price you want to trade, determine which Fibonacci line the binary option strike price is near.

The results of overlaying the Fibonacci lines on the underlying market can be very valuable to the trader. The relationship between binary option strike prices and Fibonacci lines are important because they can confirm whether the intended strike price is the best one to use for a trade. If, for example, a trader goes long a binary option strike price, but that strike price is just above a key 61.8 Fib line, it means that there is likely to be great resistance encountered. The trade success is less likely, or requires a lot more momentum than anticipated. Fib lines can confirm a choice of a binary option strike price. If the spot market has just probed above a 61.8 percent Fib line and the trade wants to go with an in-the-money strategy, choosing the strike price right below the fib line makes sense.

The most important Fibonacci ratios used in trading are 38.2 percent, 50 percent, and 61.8 percent. Fibonacci resistance lines on the day chart are the

TABLE 5.1 EUR/USD Strike Prices

Market	Expiration Date	Bid	Offer
EUR/USD > 1.4625	3-Jun-11	17.5	22.5
EUR/USD > 1.4575	3-Jun-11	18	22.5
EUR/USD > 1.4525	3-Jun-11	24.5	29.5
EUR/USD > 1.4475	3-Jun-11	31.5	37
EUR/USD > 1.4425	3-Jun-11	39.5	45
EUR/USD > 1.4375	3-Jun-11	47.5	54
EUR/USD > 1.4325	3-Jun-11	56	62
EUR/USD > 1.4275	3-Jun-11	64.5	70
EUR/USD > 1.4225	3-Jun-11	72	77

most important. Many underlying markets often have prices probing near the key day fib lines. EUR/USD provides such an example. First we locate the EUR/USD chart and notice a significant high was formed about May 9. The price action followed with a decline and formed a low. The Fibonacci tool connects the high to the low and generates the Fibonacci ratios. At the same time, viewing the EUR/USD weekly binary option strike prices (Table 5.1) showed that the 1.4675 strike price was the closest to the actual 61.8 percent Fib line, which was at 1.4572 (Figure 5.31). This is almost an exact overlay of a key Fibonacci line and a binary option strike price. The result is a confluence of confirmation that a trader loves to see from more than one technical condition. The trader looking to go long the EUR/USD would realize that a strong move was necessary to break through.

> **TIP**
>
> The binary option trade will face more resistance than usual when a strike price is near a key Fibonacci price point. It is a good idea to always check for the presence of Fibonacci patterns.

This chapter has shown that a basic form of technical analysis for the binary option trader starts when the trader identifies patterns in the price action. Those patterns reflect the shape of market sentiment and the stability of the pattern is directly related to the stability of the sentiment. Since binary option trading is focused on direction, the trader should apply pattern analysis, and initially focus on trend analysis, to increase confidence about the trading decision he or she is about to make and improve the probability of profitable results.

FIGURE 5.31   Fibonacci Lines and Binary Option Strike Price Location

References

Brown, Constance. 2008. *Fibonacci Analysis*. New York: Bloomberg Press.
Nison, Steve. 1994. *Beyond Candlesticks: New Japanese Charting Techniques Revealed*. New York: John Wiley & Sons.

CHAPTER 6

Advanced Technical Analysis: Volatility Tools

Beyond basic technical analysis of chart trend direction and chart patterns, there remains one more significant category of technical analysis that can give binary option traders an edge. It is the category of volatility tools. There are many of them. Let's take a closer look.

Defining Volatility

Let's first clarify what volatility is before delving into its technical aspects for trading. Simply put, if prices stayed stable and within a small range over any period of time, then volatility would be minimal. *Volatility* is a measure of the swings in price action and the rate of change of those swings. The trader detects volatility by seeing the market become increasingly anxious. Market anxiety can be observed first in headlines as well as the emergence of wider price swings. This is in contrast to the experience of a calm market with very little price action. Ignoring the volatility conditions of the underlying market is a recipe for misapplying binary option strategies. High volatility conditions, if ignored, will lead to applying inappropriate trading strategies. High volatility conditions are associated with larger swings in prices and therefore wider ranges. These conditions are excellent for successful application of *out-of-the-money (OTM)* and *deep-out-of-the-money (DOTM)* trades. They are more likely to work out when volatility is higher because price swings are more likely. However, extremely high volatility conditions are often used by traders as reversal signals. The reasoning is that extreme volatility reflects transient

97

conditions and the underlying market will return to average ranges of volatility. This is also known as regression to the mean. In contrast, low volatility conditions reflect a market that is clustered and is often a prelude to a breakout. There are many technical analysis tools available to the trader to monitor volatility conditions. Let's review some basic ones that ought to be applied.

Bollinger Bands

Bollinger Bands are a good first approach to mapping price volatility. They enable every trader to view volatility conditions. Bollinger Band charts have three parts. The first part is a curved line in the middle. This is a *moving average* line. The second part is a *lower band,* and the third part is an *upper band.* The bands are called Bollinger Bands because John Bollinger devised them. The upper and lower Bollinger Bands are a statistical curve that is placed around the price. In other words, they represent a special kind of boundary. The upper and lower bands actually represent a standard deviation around a moving average. The concept of standard deviation is a statistical concept used to summarize data. It's seen in most applications as a bell curve. Let's see how it can be applied to the world of trading.

A common setting of the bands is (20, 2). This means that the moving average in the middle of the bands is a 20-period moving average. It also means that the upper and lower bands are two standard deviations from the moving average. This setting translates, in simpler terms, that the price is 96 percent of the time between the two bands! If the setting was (20, 3) the Bollinger Band chart would still have a 20-period moving average in the middle, but the upper and lower band would be three standard deviations, or 99 percent from the middle. The default setting used by traders is accepted as (20, 2).

VOLATILITY MATH

For the math-minded, here is a formula for volatility.

$$\text{Vol} = 100 \sqrt{\frac{252}{n} \sum R_1^2 R_t}$$

Vol = realized volatility

N = number of trading days in the period

Rt = continuously compounded daily returns

Bollinger Bands are a popular indicator used in many markets. They enable the trader to confirm whether the price is at an upper range or resistance, and whether the price is at a lower range or support. When prices are near Bollinger Bands, they have a strong probability of pausing in their direction and reversing. This has important implications to the binary option trader because the binary option strike price may be located above, or below one of the bands. Or the binary option strike price might be right in the middle of the band. The trader needs to know where the binary option strike price is in relationship to the band to assess properly the degree of likely resistance or support that will be encountered as time moves forward.

Interpreting Bollinger Bands

Interpreting the Bollinger Band patterns (Figure 6.1) is straightforward and can be explained as a simple three-step process:

1. Notice the shape of the band.

    The bands can be narrow or wide. If the band is narrow, it means that the market is becoming undecided as to which direction to go. A narrow band becomes narrow as the range between support and resistance decreases. A band becomes wider as the range becomes wider.
2. Notice the direction of the bands.

    The band can be sideways, tilted up, or tilted down. If it is a sideways band and looks quite level, this means that the trend direction is in a pause before it resumes going up or down. If the bands are tilted up, this means that the trend is upward. If the bands are titled down, it means the trend is downward.
3. Notice the location of the price.

    The price (candles or bars) are often right on the band. If there are several candles in a row on an upper or lower band, it indicates that the market is sticky and is not ready yet to decide which way to go.

Do's and Don'ts

When noticing a narrow band, try to avoid trading it because it can suddenly move against you. It's actually a very good precondition for a breakout binary option trade. When the price has moved above the Bollinger Band, watch if it tries to come back below the band; if it does, it is an indication of a reversal down. When the price has moved below the Bollinger Band, watch if it tries

FIGURE 6.1   Basic Features of Bollinger Bands

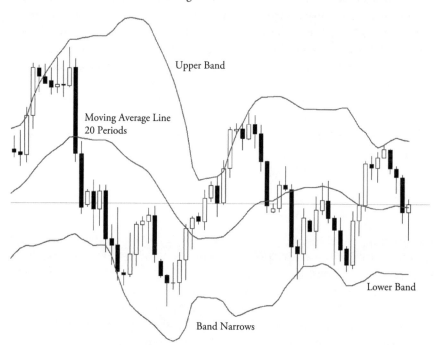

Upper Band

Moving Average Line
20 Periods

Lower Band

Band Narrows

to come back above it; if it doesn't, it is an indication of a reversal back up. Don't assume that if a price is at a Bollinger Band, it will stop there. It can stay at the band for a long time.

Bollinger Bands also provide a standard and accepted quick look at volatility. The wider the bands are, the greater the range between support and resistance. When Bollinger Bands become narrow, it is a signal of break-out potential. When Bollinger Bands are very wide, they reflect increased volatility conditions. The Bollinger Band has a standard setting of (20, 2). The number 20 represents the simple moving average, and the number 2 represents the standard deviation around the moving average. This means that the price is 96 percent of the time between the upper and lower levels. A price probing or breaking an upper or lower band signals a big change in volatility. It means the trader should be much attuned to what is going on. The price is there for a reason, and assumptions that it will reverse have to be confirmed.

An additional technique useful to traders is to put on an extra outer band at a setting of (13, 2.618). This additional setting represents 13 periods as the moving average and a 2.618 standard deviation. This means that the upper and lower bands are capturing 99 percent of the move. A price that has gone through the standard band (20, 2) and also the outer band of (13, 2.618) is at very high levels of extreme value. This is often associated with very high levels of volatility and therefore is a reversal signal.

Using Bands with Support and Resistance Lines

In our introductory section, we described the basic definition of Bollinger Bands. This section will help you identify ways to combine Bollinger Bands with other technical analysis tools to make them even more effective. The first tool that should be combined with a Bollinger Band is a support and resistance line. In many ways, a Bollinger Band acts as a kind of resistance, or support line. By its very nature, the bands are providing a boundary for the price. It is a statistical boundary and the bands are not actual price support or resistance lines. A price support and resistance line connects lows or highs of the prices in a selected time interval. When you combine Bollinger Bands and support and resistance lines, the effect can be much greater information about how strong the support or resistance is. It is always a good idea to use both Bollinger Bands and support and resistance lines.

We see that the upper Bollinger Band is coinciding almost exactly with the resistance line (Figure 6.2). When this happens the trader is more confident that there is serious and strong resistance in this area. It's important to notice that the price highs are able to go above the upper Bollinger Band. This shows that the Bollinger Bands are really a zone and should not be interpreted as a solid resistance or support area. It's important to observe what the price is doing after it penetrates the Bollinger Band. Is it returning back into the band? When this happens, it is a strong reversal condition.

Using Bands with Trend Lines

Another useful approach is to combine Bollinger Bands with trend lines. This combination works very well together (Figure 6.3).

First, we can notice that the band is fairly sideways and wide in shape. This provides more opportunity for the price to bounce around. In fact, we can see that the price came to the bottom of the bands and started turning up. It created an outer trend and then quickly shifted inward and it created an *inner trend line* and then another inner trend line. This showed a great deal of momentum. By drawing the inner trend lines, the trader can see that

FIGURE 6.2 Bollinger Bands with Support and Resistance Lines

Bollinger Bands coincide
with resistance level

Sell on
break

Sell condition as
price hugs band

the price is very bullish. In fact, the price went up to the top of the Bollinger Band. When the price is at an upper band, it is a clue that it may turn around. In this situation, the trader should wait until the price goes back and breaks the trend line to confirm a selling condition!

Let's examine a situation in which the price is entering a downward trend and the candles are sliding down the lower Bollinger Band (Figure 6.4). This kind of pattern is seen often. The price after going up then breaks its uptrend. At that point, it is a sell signal. Another sell point occurs when the price on its way down hesitates, forms a doji, and then breaks down. This is a key sell point because it shows a failure to go up.

FIGURE 6.3   Bollinger Bands and Trend Lines

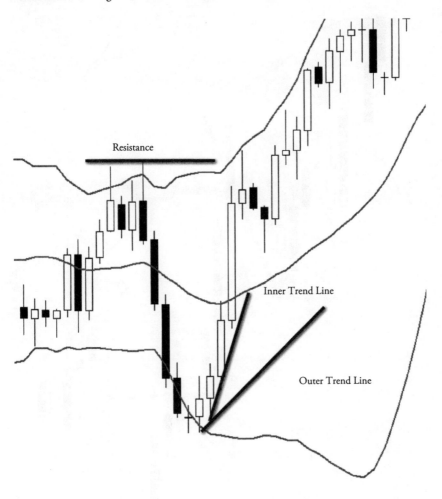

The question will arise: What are indications that a bounce back up is likely? If the price is in a downtrend line and it breaks that line, then the situation can be considered a move toward the other side. By using trend lines in combination with Bollinger Bands, the ability to locate an entry point is greatly enhanced. If the Bollinger Band is sideways and flat, it really is the best shape for binary option traders because it's the condition for a breakout trade.

FIGURE 6.4   Price Action on the Lower Bollinger Band

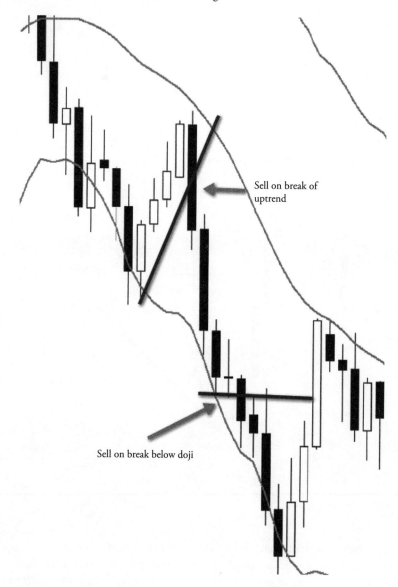

Sell on break of uptrend

Sell on break below doji

Adding Another Band with a Different Setting

To further advance your knowledge and use of Bollinger Bands, we introduce here the addition of a second band setting. The first setting is a standard, or default, setting of 20, 2. This, as you know, means, 20 periods, and two standard deviations. It captures between the two bands 96 percent of the prices. What happens if we add another band with a different setting? Another band might help us understand better what is happening with the first band! A second band setting suggested here is known as the *extended Bollinger Band (EBB)*. Its setting is (13, 2.618). This means the moving average is 13 periods and the standard deviation is nearly at 3 or 99 percent. The 2.618 is really a Fibonacci extension number.

Let's examine what it means for the trader to put on another Bollinger Band with the settings of 13, 2.618 (Figure 6.5). First, it means that the moving average, or the middle line of the Bollinger Band, is a shorter time line. Contrast this with the 20-period time line. This provides the trader a view that is nearer to the recent action. But the adjustment of the setting to 2.618 standard deviations means that the band widens to capture nearly 99 percent of the action. If we put these two settings together, we have two upper bands and two lower bands! The result is four bands. The trader should particularly focus on where the price is. If the price is beyond the inner band, which is usually the standard band setting of 20, 2, it means the price is at an extreme. But the trader using an extended Bollinger Band can see that it would be very extreme only if it went to touch or go beyond the outer band of 13, 2.618. The addition of an extended Bollinger Band is very effective in alerting the trader to a buy or sell signal. In Figure 6.5 we see that the price hit a double bottom that was sitting right on both lower bands. That represents very strong support.

Let's consider how the EBB generates price signals. For a sell signal situation, the concept is simply that if the price goes to the EBB, the trader has an extreme situation and can consider it to be a strong predictor of a reversal. If the price goes beyond the EBB and then returns below it, this is a strong sell signal.

A buy signal is straightforward. If the price goes beyond the bottom EBB and then returns above it, it is a strong buy signal!

We can clearly see in Figure 6.5 that when the price went down to the lower bands, a candle going back up followed it. This showed that the mood of the market was more bullish. Without the EBB, the trader wouldn't have an ability to confirm if the price is about to reverse.

Example of Step-by-Step Analysis

Let's pause and reflect on the technical analysis process so far, evolving toward placing a binary option trade (Figure 6.6). The flow of analysis starts with an initial technical scan of fundamental market conditions. A second phase consists

FIGURE 6.5   Buy and Sell Signals with Extended Bollinger Bands

Extended Bollinger Band
setting = (13,2.618)

Strong double bottom

FIGURE 6.6   Technical Analysis Process Leading to Binary Option Trades

of a thorough checking and ranking of trend conditions. The analytical process continues by checking the presence of sideways, or ranging, markets. At this point, a close look at chart patterns is in order. Some underlying markets look better than others and will appeal to the trader. Once you select the underlying market(s) to trade, the challenge is to find the binary option strike price that matches the pattern. Then place your trade. Let's explore these steps with more scrutiny.

Step 1: Scan the Fundamental Market Conditions

The initial technical analysis scanning process starts with a review of the most important market complexes. They include, but are not limited to the USDX, gold, oil, the Shanghai Index, SPX, and so on.

The goal of the scan is to evaluate the technical conditions in these important markets. The conditions include, but are not limited to trends, momentum, resistance, support, and volatility.

While there isn't one single method to conduct the technical scan, the initial scan should include multiple time frames. Multiple time frames need to be reviewed from the weekly and daily to the four-hour patterns to gain a sense about any changes in the mood of the market. The four-hour pattern provides a good interim time period. It reflects most recent market reactions, and allows the trader to still review the price action over several days. The key point here is to never review only one time frame. Upon performing the scans, ask yourself what is interesting that strikes you. Interesting patterns noticed by the trader are very important. This is also known as the blink effect. It means one can recognize binary trading opportunities within seconds!

FIGURE 6.7   Key Markets to Scan

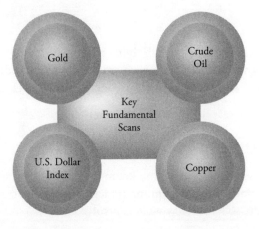

Step 2: Check and Rank Trend Conditions

The focus of analysis here is on ranking the trend conditions. Trends can be just starting, strong, and stable. Of course, they can also begin to show weakening. These conditions, once detected, will help the trader match the binary option strategy that best fits the changing trend conditions.

As noted earlier, a very good charting tool for assessing trend conditions is the three-line break chart. This charting focuses exclusively on detecting the strength of the trend. In any case, no matter which charts you are using, ranking the trend conditions is a useful technique. Besides using three-line break charts, a commonly accepted measure of trend strength is the 50-day moving average. If the underlying market is probing the 50-day moving average, it is a signal of a change in the trend. Also, for each underlying market, rank the trend for the weekly, daily, and four-hour chart. A rank of one means the trend has just begun after reversing the previous trend. A rank of two means it's into the beginning of a new trend. A rank of three means it's a stable trend (usually approaching a 37 to 45 degree angle). A rank of four means it's accelerating; five means it's almost parabolic.

Step 3: Check If a Sideways Ranging Market Exists

If a market is not trending, it must be in a range. Markets in a range provide excellent binary trading opportunities. So, just as it was important to rank the trending markets, it's important to rank those markets that are ranging. Ask yourself: Have there been multiple tests of resistance or support?

Is there a breakout pattern forming?

Step 4: Choose Underlying Markets to Trade

While there are more than 20 underlying markets to choose, the simple fact is that most people should start with trading only a handful. The choice of what to trade should be based on conclusions derived from Step 1 to Step 3.

Step 5: Evaluate Volatility Conditions

Once you choose the underlying market to trade, it's important to look at the volatility conditions. Many beginning traders ignore this phase. We have not covered this step, so let's review what is involved.

These five basic steps provide a firm foundation for assessing trading conditions. The trader should always be sure that she has participated in each step. The effect of using each step is that it will minimize misunderstanding market conditions.

VIX: The Fear Index

In addition to Bollinger Bands, another tool that binary option traders should know about and use is the *VIX Index*. The words *fear* and *risk aversion* reflect bearish sentiment. But even more importantly, they are evidence of a herding behavior. The crowd has joined the sentiment wave of fear. It's a powerful event and moves markets and creates trading opportunities.

Here is what the CBOE says about VIX:

> The CBOE Volatility Index (VIX) is a key measure of market expectations of near-term volatility conveyed by S&P 500 stock index option prices. Since its introduction in 1993, VIX has been considered by many to be the world's premier barometer of investor sentiment and market volatility.

What is important about the VIX is its use as a contrarian indicator for the S&P 500. The inverse correlation often approaches 90 percent (Table 6.1). The S&P 500 as an underlying market is one of the most important as it affects many other markets. Trading the S&P 500 depends not only on basic charting analysis, it requires tracking emotions and the mood of the market.

So if a binary option trader wants to select a direction for trading the S&P, it's a very good idea to first check volatility. Historically, the inverse correlation relationship between the VIX and S&P 500 has been quite high, reaching to over 85 percent in the opposite direction (Figure 6.8). As with other instruments, there is never a linear correlation. There are times when the VIX and the S&P 500 can move together.

TABLE 6.1 VIX Futures Indexes Have Historically Been Negatively Correlated with the S&P 500

Date	S&P 500 VIX Correlation
12/17/14	−0.8539
6/24/15	−0.8812

Data source: Bloomberg Financial LP.

FIGURE 6.8   VIX Movements and the S&P 500

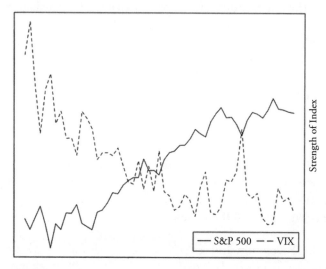

Source: Bloomberg Financial, L.P.

How should the VIX relationship to the S&P 500 be used? Its most important use is confirming whether extreme conditions are in place in the market. If the VIX is rising fast, the S&P 500 is likely falling fast. These are transient conditions, and the binary option trader, who is looking for a directional bet for a few days, has to be careful. But the VIX isn't only for the S&P 500. Since its introduction, there are a large number of volatility indexes for other underlying markets that provide indicators of whether those markets are at low or high extremes in volatility. For example, there is a VIX for the Brent Crude oil market, which is also contrarian. Its symbol is OVX. We can see that when the OVX hit highs, it was a leading indicator of a decline in crude (Figure 6.9). West Texas oil has its own volatility index— OIV (Figure 6.10). Gold spot has a volatility index version with the symbol GVZ. Binary option traders who trade gold directions use it to see volatility conditions (Figure 6.11). Silver, like gold has its own volatility index with the symbol VXSLV (Figure 6.12).

The FTSE index provides an excellent example of the contrarian relationship between extremes in VIX and direction. The symbol VFTSE is the VIX for the FTSE (Figure 6.13). The DAX30 has a VIX counterpart in the symbol VDAX (Figure 6.14). The key volatility indexes associated with the binary option underlying markets are important to follow. They will enable the

FIGURE 6.9 Crude Oil and Its Volatility Index (OVX)

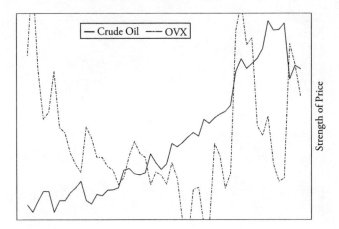

Source: Bloomberg Financial, L.P.

FIGURE 6.10 West Texas Oil and Its Volatility Index (OIV)

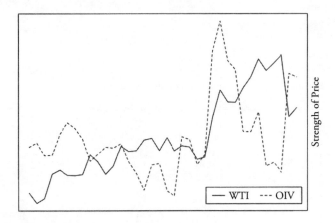

Source: Bloomberg Financial, L.P.

trader to spot opportunities and extremes in markets otherwise difficult to detect. Use the different VIXs as a barometer of market sentiment. It doesn't matter if there is no underlying binary option market to trade. They do help. For example, the Hang Seng index has its own VIX (CHIX) and it provides an ability to monitor sentiment on the Chinese markets (Figure 6.15). More volatility indexes in the future are likely to be developed. A good idea is to always inquire whether a key index has its own VIX version.

FIGURE 6.11   Gold Spot and Its Volatility Index (GVZ)

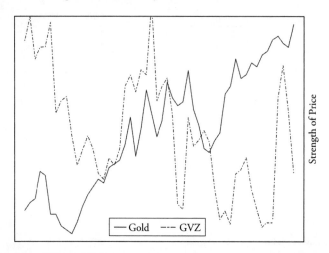

Source: Bloomberg Financial, L.P.

FIGURE 6.12   Silver Spot and Its Volatility Index (VXSLV)

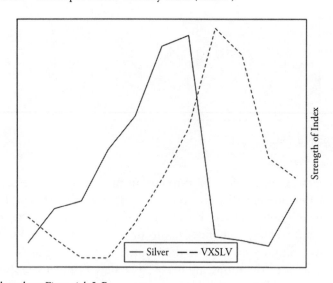

Source: Bloomberg Financial, L.P.

FIGURE 6.13 FTSE and Its Volatility Index (VFTSE)

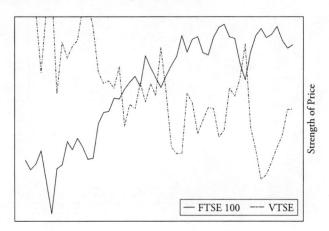

Source: Bloomberg Financial, L.P.

FIGURE 6.14 The DAX 30 and Its Volatility Index (VDAX)

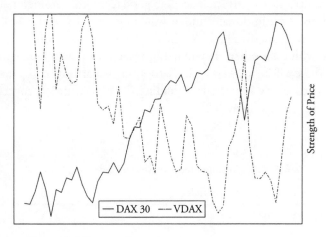

Source: Bloomberg Financial, L.P.

The overall value of knowing the volatility of the underlying markets is to use it as a confirming indicator of breakout conditions. Without any volatility, there would be little information about the conditions of market opinion. Extremes in volatility can be considered valuable information events as well as contrarian signals that the market direction is about to reverse. While this

FIGURE 6.15   Hang Seng Index and the Volatility Index (CHIX)

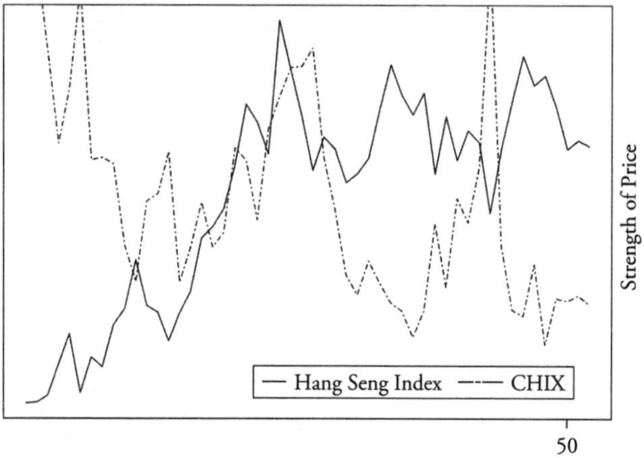

Source: Bloomberg Financial, L.P.

relationship is never perfect, it acts as a good technical barometer of sentiment conditions. An additional value of watching several global volatility indexes is to see which are diverging. While the foreign markets often move in coincidence with each other, they may not react with the same magnitude to an event. There will be markets with relatively lower volatility compared to others. This is particularly important in trading the binary option contracts for the equity indexes (see Table 6.2).

TABLE 6.2   Volatility Index of Several Underlying Markets

Underlying Volatility Index	Symbol
FTSE 100 Volatility	VFTSE
DAX Volatility	DAX 30
HANG SENG INDEX	CHIX
NIFTY 50	INDIA 50
CRUDE OIL	OVX
NYMEX WTI	OIV
GOLD	GVZ
SILVER	VXSLV

> **TIP**
>
> Check the latest VIX data at https://www.cboe.com/micro/volatility/pricecharts
> .aspx.

Option Volatility and Sentiment: Put/Call Ratios

A long established class of volatility indicators is known as the *put/call ratio*. It is a classic sentiment indicator. The concept is that when traders are bearish, they buy puts. When they are bullish about direction, they buy calls. As a result, extremes in sentiment can be detected. How does a trader know when the sentiment is skewed in favor of puts or calls? There are several ways of measuring sentiment extremes. First, when the sentiment is predominantly bearish, there is naturally more contract volume of puts than that of calls. The result is known as the *put/call ratio*. This is the volume of put options/volume of call options. Once again, the concept of volatility or extreme variation in a pattern comes into play. The key step in relationship to put/call ratios is to identify when these ratios are at extremes. Put/call premium ratios are reliable gauges of the skew of opinion.

A second, valuable form of the put/call ratio is the comparison of the implied volatility of the puts divided by the implied volatility of the calls. The reasoning is: if buying an at-the-money put is more expensive than an at-the-money call, the market is more bearish.

The binary option trader can use a variety of sources to locate put/call ratios for a particular underlying market. One common source is the futures market. Even if you are not trading futures contracts, the value of the put/call information is worthy of review and is available by viewing the futures options contracts at the CME, CBOT, NYMEX, and other futures trading exchanges. A quick guide to whether fear or greed is dominant in the market can be seen at www.money.cnn.com/data/fear-and-greed.

Their Fear and Greed index monitors seven factors: put/call ratio, VIX, the McClellan Volume Summation Index, stock price strength, haven demand, market momentum, and junk bond demand.

Sector Put/Call Ratios

Just like the case with the VIX, for every underlying market offering binary options, there is also a corresponding *sector index*, or group of funds that provide option data on the sentiment regarding that market. This is also important to review because the sentiment on an underlying market may be related, or not, to the overall market it is a part of. Once an underlying market is being considered for trading the binaries, an important additional step in shaping the directional trade is to check on the put/call ratios of the sector. How can this be done? To be able to do this, the trader can locate exchange traded funds (ETFs) that offer options on them and then determine the associated put/call volume. The CBOE is a great site for locating this information.

Let's look at some examples of using ETFs and the put/call ratio in preparing to trade gold binaries. One can look at GLD, a gold ETF, and at the same time check the put/call ratio. During the period shown in Figure 6.16, gold had reached new highs and sold off only to recover again. The put/call ratio for gold on 0.9947 shows a neutral mood for the market and is leaning neither bullish nor bearish. The binary option trader has to use this sentiment information to confirm which way he wants to trade.

Similarly, if a trader was looking to put on binary options on the oil market, USO, an ETF on oil provides option sentiment data to use (Figure 6.17). In addition to scanning the USO chart, the put/call ratio provides a gauge on the mood of traders on this market. Oil had reached highs because of

FIGURE 6.16   Gold ETF

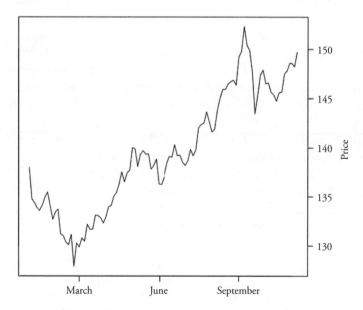

Source: Bloomberg Financial, L.P.

FIGURE 6.17 USO ETF

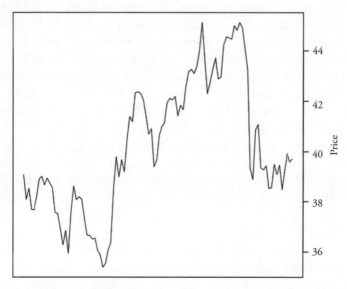

Source: Bloomberg Financial, L.P.

Middle East turbulence, and then sold off. The chart looks like a sideways action. Looking at the put/call ratio, the trader finds a 1.0102 ratio, indicating slightly bearish sentiment.

There should be no doubt that a greater insight into the sentiment of the market is gained by examining options on the ETF.

Volatility Smiles

When markets are leaning bullish or bearish, the extent of the shift in sentiment to one side may be predictive of price action that follows in the days ahead. Option traders try to detect the strength of bearish and bullish sentiment by looking at volatility smiles. The *volatility smile* is simply a graphic of the volatility surface. It reflects an imbalance in the implied volatilities of an option at the same strike price. Either the implied volatility of puts at the same strike price is greater than the implied volatility of calls at that strike price or vice-versa. If the market crowd were neutral in regard to direction, there would be no skew. It would be a perfect smile! But that hardly ever occurs. The more experienced binary option traders may want to use volatility smiles to see which way the market is leaning. It provides more evidence, not necessarily where the market will go, but where the opinion pool is clustering.

When the volatility smile is extremely skewed to puts or calls, it can be interpreted as confirming a strategy to follow the skew. Alternatively, it can also be interpreted as representing an exaggerated condition and a reversal is coming. On its own, a volatility smile cannot be used as the only source of a confirmation on direction. It's also important to locate the volatility smile for weekly or one-month durations as its relevance to binary option decisions declines when the smiles are using longer-term time frames.

An effective way to apply volatility smiles to binary option trading is to evaluate the presence of a smile or a skew as a way of confirming the mood of the market. Then compare the results of the review with your own opinion. Is your binary option bet going with the skew or betting that it will reverse?

Let's look at a snapshot of some volatility smiles and relate them to the mood of the market at that time.

The EUR/USD on May 30 showed a volatility smile that is leaning to the put side. This is very bearish. In fact, Figure 6.18 shows that the one-week smile is much more bearish than the one-month smile, because the implied volatility curve is shifted upward.

FIGURE 6.18 EUR/USD One-Week versus Three-Month Volatility Smiles

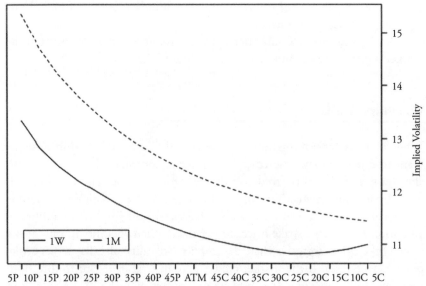

5P 10P 15P 20P 25P 30P 35P 40P 45P ATM 45C 40C 35C 30C 25C 20C 15C 10C 5C

Source: Bloomberg Financial, L.P.

FIGURE 6.19   AUD/USD Three-Month Volatility Smile

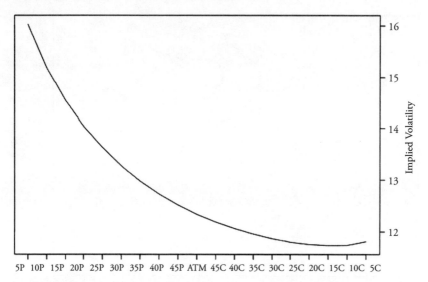

5P 10P 15P 20P 25P 30P 35P 40P 45P ATM 45C 40C 35C 30C 25C 20C 15C 10C 5C

Source: Bloomberg Financial, L.P.

The AUD/USD pair shows a very steep bias to puts. This would make a binary trader think twice about going long the AUD/USD. An appropriate strategy when the volatility smile is skewed so far is to go with the crowd with a deep-in-the-money strategy (Figure 6.19).

The GBP/USD volatility smile also shows, compared to the AUD/USD, a steeper lean to the put side (Figure 6.20). The USD/CHF volatility smile here is interesting because it shows, in contrast to the EUR/USD (Figure 6.18), a bit more of a sentiment for calls, but still very bearish (Figure 6.21).

The USD/CAD pair is the only one of the majors that has a smile that is favoring the call side, showing a very strong bias for a stronger dollar (Figure 6.22). Traders looking for a stronger Canadian dollar because of stronger oil would think twice about it.

The USD/JPY volatility smile was almost the only one close to being balanced and showing a normal smile (Figure 6.23). This correlates with a sideways action and, in fact, a normal smile supports a breakout strategy since the market is not showing any domination regarding direction.

Our last volatility smile is the GBP/JPY cross pair. We see a very strong preference for a weakening of this pair. Once again seeing this, the choice facing the trading is to either be contrarian and go the other way, or join the crowd (Figure 6.24).

FIGURE 6.20   GBP/USD Three-Month Volatility Smile

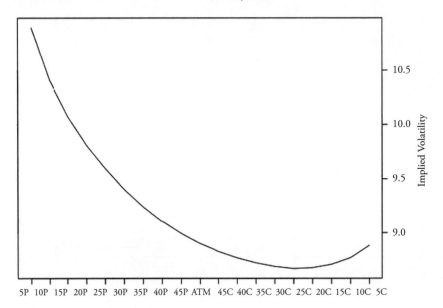

Source: Bloomberg Financial, L.P.

FIGURE 6.21   USD/CHF Three-Month Volatility Smile

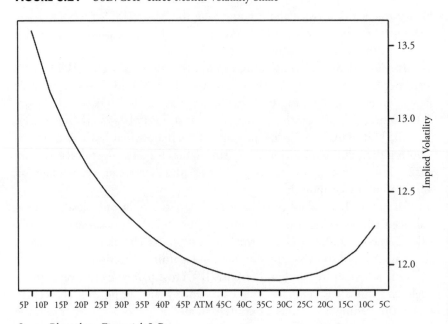

Source: Bloomberg Financial, L.P.

FIGURE 6.22 USD/CAD Volatility Smile

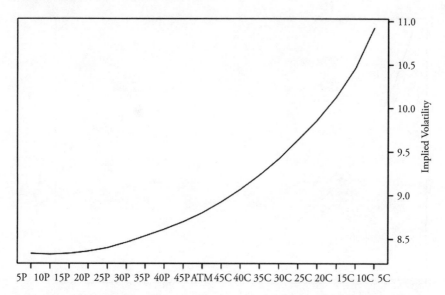

5P 10P 15P 20P 25P 30P 35P 40P 45P ATM 45C 40C 35C 30C 25C 20C 15C 10C 5C

Source: Bloomberg Financial, L.P.

FIGURE 6.23 USD/JPY Volatility Smile

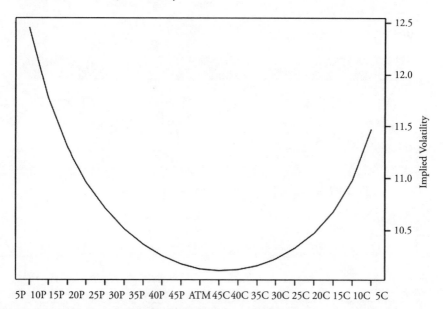

5P 10P 15P 20P 25P 30P 35P 40P 45P ATM 45C 40C 35C 30C 25C 20C 15C 10C 5C

Source: Bloomberg Financial, L.P.

FIGURE 6.24   GBP/JPY Volatility Smile

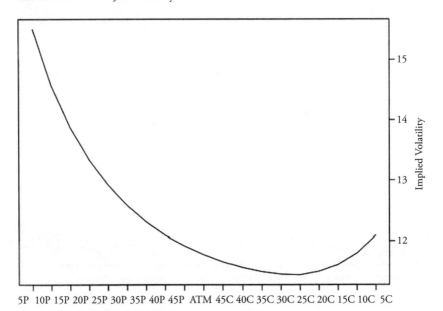

5P 10P 15P 20P 25P 30P 35P 40P 45P ATM 45C 40C 35C 30C 25C 20C 15C 10C 5C

Source: Foundation for the Study of Cycles, Inc.

FIGURE 6.25   S&P 500 Cycle

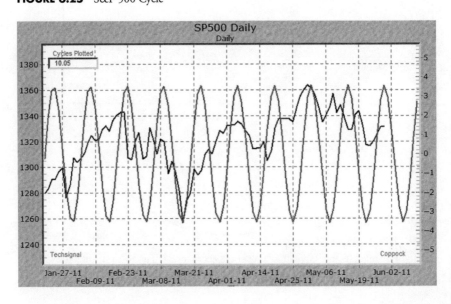

FIGURE 6.26 EUR/USD Cycle

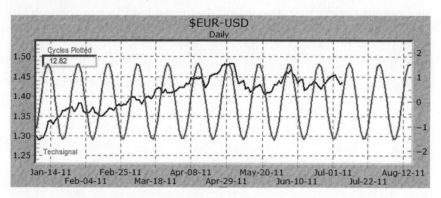

Source: Foundation for the Study of Cycles, Inc.

The difficulty with volatility smiles is that it takes special software offered by third parties to generate the visuals. They are, however, available for the more sophisticated trader through special software and applications. Also, the more quant-oriented traders can generate their own volatility smiles from grabbing option data from the web. In any case, traders who access volatility smiles will find it a useful tool to gain an edge.

Fear of Recession

The emergence out of the financial collapse of 2008 occurred in 2015 as the United States fully recovered in its financial condition. The increase in interest rates on December 16 signaled a shift in the confidence about the U.S. economy. The statement of the FOMC on December 16 is perhaps one of the most important statements that traders should study. (See the full statement in Chapter 4). In reading it, the Federal Reserve is signaling what it will look at in deciding future interest rate increases. A focus on inflation and whether it will be near 2 percent is one important parameter.

The decision to raise rates, however, introduces a new fear: *fear of a recession.* If the U.S. economic recovery weakens or stalls, it will generate a fear of recession and increased volatility in the U.S. dollar, gold, and related markets. The trader could have an edge if they understand and monitor that one of the indicators of a recession will be the shape of the yield curve. An inverse yield curve is accepted as a strong indicator of a recession (Estrella and Trubin 2006). When the yield curve inverts, it is generally accepted as a predictor of a coming recession. An inverted yield curve is the difference (spread) between the 10-year Treasury note and the three-month Treasury bill. We can see in Table 6.3 that the probability of a recession is greater than 50 percent when the spread gets above −1.00.

The spread as of December 17, the day after the Federal Reserve raised rates by 25 basis points was 1.985. This value is a result of the calculation:

U.S. Treasury 10-Year Bonds (2.2395) − (U.S. Treasury Three-Month Bill (0.2545.) = 1.985.

It is very far away from the negative value necessary to signal a recession. Nevertheless, it's a good idea for the trader to keep track of this relationship from time to time.

A sentiment-based component for predicting a recession that should be used is the frequency of the word "recession" mentioned in Google search engines. If the frequency increases, it is a clue that there is increased concern about it.

TABLE 6.3   Estimated Recession Probabilities for Probit Model Using the Yield Curve Spread (Four Quarters Ahead)

Recession Probability (%)	Value of Spread (% Points)
5	1.21
10	0.76
15	0.46
20	0.22
25	0.02
30	−0.17
40	−0.50
50	−0.82
60	−1.13
70	−1.46
80	−1.85
90	−2.40

Note: The yield curve spread is defined as the spread between the interest rates on the 10-year Treasury notes and the three-month Treasury bill.

Source: Federal Reserve Bank of New York, *Current Issues in Economics and Finance*, 2, (7), June 1996; Arturo Estrella and Frederic S. Mishkin, "The Yield Curve as a Predictor of U.S. Recessions." Accessed January 22, 2016 at http://core.ac.uk/download/files/153/6867393.pdf.

Tracking Money Supply as an Indicator of Growth

The fear of a recession in the United States is likely to be linked to a change in the money supply. If the money supply is insufficient, then the economy is likely to not have the liquidity necessary to stimulate growth. After the 2008 crisis, banks reduced their lending, which froze the economy. The Great Recession that followed the 2008 collapse was very long substantially because of the lack of money growth. The recession officially began in December 2007 and ended in June 2009. Roughly 80 percent of the money supply is determined by banks providing credit and loans and 20 percent is provided by the United States government. The trader now has the benefit of access to good data on the money supply. It is published by the Center for Financial Stability (www.centeroffinancialstablity). The trader should look at the measure called CFS Divisia M4, "which is the broadest and most important measure of money." M4 includes notes and coins and bank accounts. It is not a coincidence that as this broad measure of money supply increases, the financial condition of the economy also increases. It is a good idea to keep track of this important M4 measure.

FIGURE 6.27 M4 Money Supply

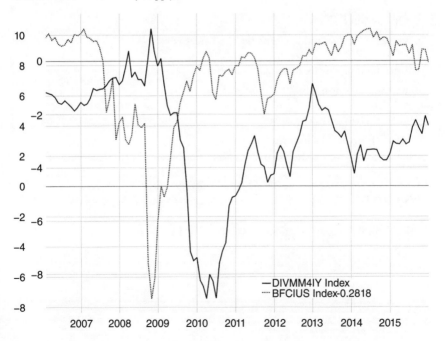

Reviewing the Tools

In this chapter, we've seen how to use several advanced technical analysis tools, including Bollinger Bands, the VIX Index, put/call ratios, and volatility smiles. We also reviewed how to track an emerging fear of recession using U.S. Treasury data. Lastly, we saw how cycle indicators can also work in the trader's favor. These tools, combined with those discussed in the basic technical analysis chapter, form a solid foundation for understanding what it takes to trade binary options successfully.

Look Online

For more information on tools for advanced technical analysis, here is a list of online resources to explore:

Commodity-based ETF options:
www.cboe.com/micro/commodity/introduction.aspx

List of Currency ETFs and ETNs:
http://etf.about.com/od/foreignetfs/a/List_of_Currency_ETFs.htm

Options on ETFs
www.cboe.com/Products/optionsOnETFs.aspx

Introduction to VIX Futures and Options:
www.cboe.com/micro/VIX/vixintro.aspx

CBOE Daily Market Statistics:
www.cboe.com/data/mktstat.aspx

Reference

Estrella, Arturo, and Mary R. Trubin. 2006. "The Yield Curve as a Leading Indicator: Some Practical Issues." *Current Issues in Economics and Finance* 12 (5, July/August): 1–7.

CHAPTER 7

Binary Option Trading Strategies

This chapter provides a review and sampling with real-world conditions in which basic binary option trading strategies combine and build upon fundamental, technical, and sentiment analyses. These examples act as case studies for learning how markets react to different events. Try to compare the trading strategies and actions reviewed here with your own approach to market conditions described. As always, once an underlying market is selected, the challenge is to determine the most highly probable winning binary strategy to apply. This chapter will help you meet that challenge. We first review core strategies and then explore trading examples.

The Core Strategies

There are many strategy variations, but there are basically seven major binary option trading strategies that provide the set of options to respond to most global market-related events.

1. In-the-money (ITM)
2. Deep-in-the-money (DITM)
3. At-the-money (ATM)
4. Out-of-the-money (OTM)
5. Deep-out-of-the-money (DOOM)
6. Range trades
7. Breakout trades

In no uncertain terms, every trader who is considering binary option trading needs to understand and master these strategies and determine when they apply. We explore them in a variety of examples in this chapter.

In-the-Money or Deep-in-the-Money

Consider the scenario of a trader recognizing a trending market condition. What strategy works in this case? If the trend is strong and the headlines seem to be screaming at you, one can sense momentum in the markets. Such conditions provide confirmation for an *in-the-money* strategy, which is a trend-following approach. After scanning the headlines, check if the trend strength continues. A good gauge is to see if the trend line is approaching a 37- to 45-degree angle, or whether the price just broke through its 50-day moving average. Ask yourself: Is the trend being confirmed by a sequence of new daily highs or new daily lows? It is a good idea to use price break charts to quickly visualize trend strength. If the answer is confirming a bull or bear trending condition, a DITM trade makes a lot of sense. Such a strategy reflects confidence that the trend direction will continue to be strong. While the term *deep-in-the-money* is very subjective, it is reasonable to consider trades that risk $75–$85 to be deep-in-the-money. They are priced high by the market because the expected probability that they will settle as a winner is high. The trader putting on a DITM is following or joining the crowd. If it is a bullish strategy (Figure 7.1), the binary strike price is priced near 80 ask. If it is a bear strategy, it is selling and receiving the bid price, which is a resistance leg above the spot price with an ask price in the range of 20 to 14 (Figure 7.2). The trader should note that the distance of the binary strike price from the spot price in binaries that are priced at 75 to 85 are often near 2 percent. That means it takes a big market move to lose those positions.

FIGURE 7.1 Model of Buying a Deep-in-the-Money Binary Option

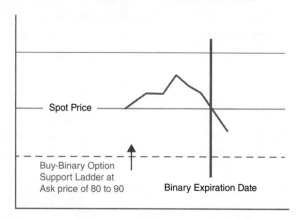

FIGURE 7.2 Model of Selling a Deep-in-the-Money Binary Option

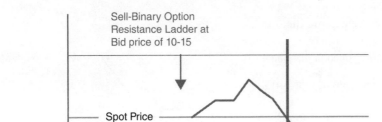

Sell-Binary Option
Resistance Ladder at
Bid price of 10-15

Spot Price

Binary Expiration Date

At-the-Money or Near-the-Money

For market conditions that point to the weakening of a trend and a possible momentum move, follow an *at-the-money (ATM)* strategy. An ATM contract is priced around $45 to $55 and this reflects a bit more market uncertainty. But if the ATM is riding with the trend direction, it is a safer play than a similarly priced binary option contract that is embedded in a sideways action. It also provides a potential return of almost 100 percent if it is settled in-the-money by Friday expiration. An *at-* or *near-the-money* binary option play can also be in response to a sideways pattern if the price is still hovering near its support or resistance level. Think of at-the-money as a bet on a bounce. It works if the market has enough energy in it to move the price out of its pattern. Binary option trades that offer higher or lower trading decisions only are in fact at-the-money trades.

Out-of-the-Money and Deep-Out-of-the Money

At the other extreme of strategies for playing the trend is an *out-of-the-money (OTM)* trade. An OTM trade of a trending underlying market is a bet that the trend will not only continue but will be able to sharply rise. A *deep-out-of-the-money (DOOM)* binary play is a long shot and an anticipation trade (Figure 7.3). The trader is going for a high-roller return and is willing to take the risk. Let's look at some real-time examples of strategic and tactical thinking in shaping the binary option trading strategy.

FIGURE 7.3   Deep-Out-of-the-Money Binary Trade

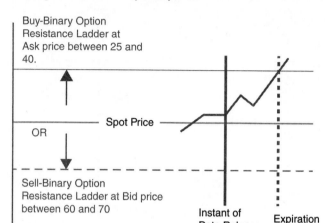

Range Traders

The range trade has as a distinctive feature one in which the trade is immediately half correct. In a range trade, one cannot be wrong on both strike prices. The range trade has as its feature selling an upper resistance strike price, and buying a lower support strike price (Figure 7.4). The wider the range, the more probable the price will stay within the range. The risk of the range trade is half the sum of the risks of both legs. The reward of the range trade is that the trader keeps the amount he sold for at the bid price, and wins 100-ask price.

FIGURE 7.4   Binary Option Range Trade

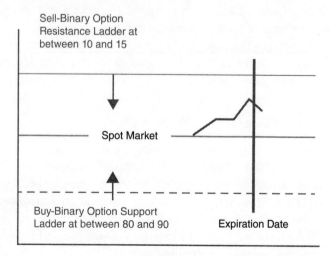

Breakout Trades

The breakout trade is the inverse of the range trade. The trader selects a range, an upper and lower strike price, and bets that the price will settle outside the range. It doesn't matter whether the price breaks through the upper resistance strike price or the lower resistance strike price. The reward or profit will be the same.

The breakout trade is essentially a play on volatility (Figure 7.5). The trader isn't betting on direction. She is simply anticipating that the move will be big enough to break through the selected range.

The breakout trade is ideal for trading key economic data releases such as the NFP report because these releases move the markets.

It takes time to become adept at matching price patterns with the best binary strategy. Figure 7.6 is a quick guide for finding the binary strategy most appropriate to the identified market condition.

World Events and Binary Trades

Applying binary option strategies to real market conditions is where the trader will gain experience and sharpen his or her skills. The beauty of weekly binary option trading is that at the start of every week, the trader has the opportunity to observe how the market has reset its balance of fears and detect whether there have been any shifts in sentiment. The binary trader is in effect a trader of world events. The following examples will help reinforce your understanding of binary trading.

FIGURE 7.5 Breakout Trade

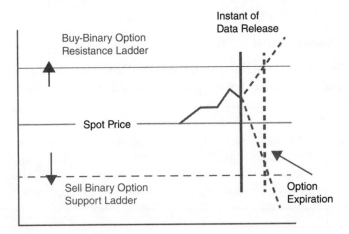

FIGURE 7.6 Summary of Trading Strategy and Market Conditions

Market Condition	Strength	Binary Strategy
Trending	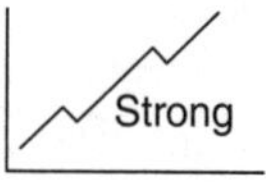 Strong	Buy Deep-in-the-Money
	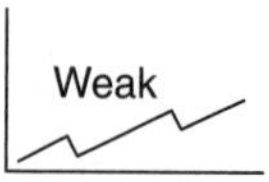 Weak	Buy or Sell At-the-Money
	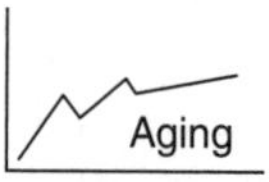 Aging	Sell Out-of-the-Money
Parabolic	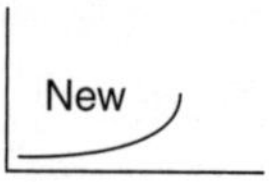 New	Buy At-the-Money
	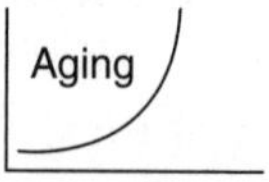 Aging	Sell At-the-Money Sell Out-of-the-Money
Sideways	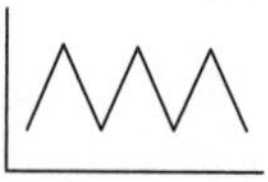	Sell Strangle

Gold as a Fundamental and Fear Play

Gold offers examples of how two fundamental forces set the stage for binary option trading. The first force is gold fear of inflation, and the second force is gold as a haven basket in times of crisis. Over the years, many gold price patterns reflect these two forces. Let's take a closer look.

The week of April 18, 2011, is our first case. During that week, gold price action patterns presented a mixed binary option trading opportunity as shown in Figure 7.7. The debt crisis at that time in Europe also became reflected in the difference between the yields of the German versus the Greek bonds (see Figure 7.8).

FIGURE 7.7 Hour Gold Spot Price During Greek Crisis from April 18 to April 23, 2011

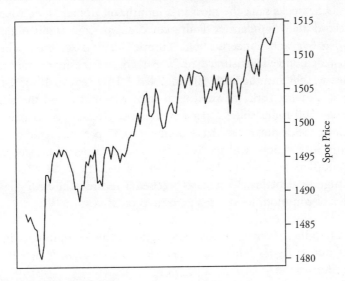

Source: Bloomberg Financial, L.P.

FIGURE 7.8 Germany versus Greek Bond Yields

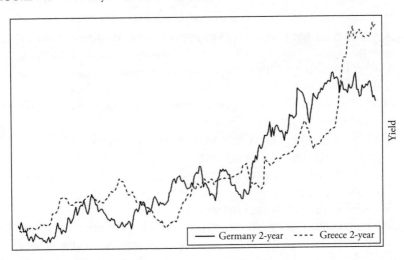

Source: Bloomberg Financial, L.P.

The week began with a big bang. The Standard & Poor's rating agency announced a lowering of the ratings on the U.S. bonds. The announcement triggered a market selloff in the equity markets and increased bullish sentiment on gold. A Bloomberg.com headline and article reflected what happened:

Stocks Sink on U.S. Credit Outlook as Euro Falls on Debt Crises

U.S. stocks sank the most in a month, oil slid and gold rose to a record after Standard & Poor's cut the American credit outlook to negative and concern about Europe's debt crises grew. Greek two-year bond yields surged to 20 percent for the first time since at least 1998 and the S&P 500 tumbled 1.1 percent to 1,305.14 at 4 P.M. in New York, its worst drop since March 16, and the Stoxx Europe 600 Index slid 1.7 percent. Ten-year Treasury notes gained, sending yields down four basis points to 3.37 percent, amid speculation S&P's move will motivate lawmakers to pass a budget that requires less borrowing. The euro lost 1.4 percent to $1.4234 and Portuguese debt-insurance costs reached a record. The S&P GSCI index of commodities slid 1.2 percent as oil sank.

Based on these events, the following real-time binary option trading alert was sent out in Agora Financial's *Strategic Currency Trading* newsletter, on Monday, April 18:

Action Alert: Playing Market Fears for a Chance at 72 Percent Gains or More

This morning, there is a mix of fears. Fear of inflation, fear of a China slowdown, fear of Eurozone financial instability centered around Greece. This translates into risk aversion—and the underlying market benefiting greatly from this sentiment is GOLD. June Comex Gold is near historic highs, and the fears that are driving these highs are not likely to abate. So the first play this week is ride the wave and BUY a gold binary option. In particular, I'm looking at the 1487.5 binary. With the gold spot market at 1484, it doesn't have to go much further to get us more than double-digit returns! [See Figure 7.7.]

Trade Action to Take: Buy a Nadex weekly gold 1487.5 binary at market.

Ordinarily, weekly gold binaries expire on Friday at 1:30 P.M. But Nadex is closed this Friday. So with the 1487.5 strike price virtually at the money, we have the ability to get a 72 percent net return in four days! But if you have less risk appetite but still want to ride the gold sentiment, you can buy a binary with a 1467.5 strike. This play is deep-in-the-money—meaning gold would have to go $17 below current spot for this binary option play to be wrong. Of course, it costs more with the current ask near $85. This is because the market has an 85 percent expectation of success. So this is not a high-roller play, but more of a portfolio strategy approach. After all, a 15 percent return in four days isn't bad!

Feeling bolder? Take a binary with a higher strike price—the 1497.5. At a current offer of $46, you have a chance to more than double your money!

Optional Trade Action to Take: Conservative traders can buy a Nadex weekly gold 1467.5 binary at market. More speculative traders can buy the Nadex weekly 1497.5 binary.

This alert employed a simple strategy of joining the gold crowd on Monday morning. There are several strategies placed in motion. This first is a deep-in-the-money play at 1467.5, an ATM at 1487.5, and an OTM at 1497.5; all rode the bullish wave and settle in-the-money, paying out $100 per unit on costs of $46 and $85. These trades had a potential total return near 17 percent and 117 percent. Adding a deeper out-of-the-money trade would, of course, result in an even greater return. The Nadex offer on $1507.5 gold was $34 on Monday. The collective wisdom of the crowd thought that there was only a 34 percent probability that gold underlying would be above that level by Friday (Table 7.1). They turned out to be very wrong!

While most traders focus on the technical market conditions at the moment of the trade, understanding binary option trading from a technical level is really not enough. The crucial factor is the mind-set of the trader. This is when emotional, as well as visual, intelligence comes into play. Putting on a binary option trade is more than implementing a technical strategy. The trade carries with it the trader's subjective interpretation of the strength of the sentiment. That is often an intuitive feeling. In our gold example, that morning's sudden selloff of gold represented something unexpected, and at the same time, it was familiar. The familiar part was the reaction process of the market. If you play a sudden event, and the move is in response to serious new information, the market will react. But the experienced trader will not always expect a selloff. If the news was so strong, it creates new conditions, and therefore, the price is likely not to reverse that quickly.

TABLE 7.1 Gold Binary Option Contracts for April 18, 2011 (April 21, 2011 Expiration)

Market	Bid	Offer
Gold (June) > 1517.5 (1:30 P.M.)	17.5	22.5
Gold (June) > 1507.5 (1:30 P.M.)	28.52	34
Gold (June) > 1497.5 (1:30 P.M.)	42.5	48.5
Gold (June) > 1487.5 (1:30 P.M.)	58	64
Gold (June) > 1477.5 (1:30 P.M.)	71.5	77
Gold (June) > 1467.5 (1:30 P.M.)	81.5	86.5
Gold (June) > 1457.5 (1:30 P.M.)	88.5	93

Of course, gold became very bearish as quantitative easing ended and U.S. interest rates increased on December 16, 2015. Gold bulls will have to wait for periods of a slowdown in the U.S. economy. The Paris terrorist attacks of November 14 provided another classical example of gold triggering a temporary haven.

Gold rose, in a haven response as markets opened the following Monday (Figure 7.9). The history of market moves in response to sudden events has demonstrated that such events generate an immediate reaction, but then is followed by a significant retracement. A contrarian gold binary play was in order and was placed.

FIGURE 7.9 Gold in Response to Paris Attacks

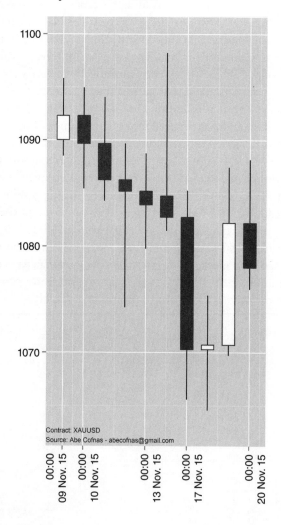

TABLE 7.2 Gold Binary Option Play in Response to Paris Terror Events

Underlying Market/ Binary Contract	Direction of Trade	Expiration Date	Settlement Price	Result
Gold (Dec) > 1104.5 (1:30 P.M.)	Sell	FRI NOV 20 13:30 EST	1074.2	WIN
Gold (Dec) > 1074 (1:30 P.M.)	Sell	FRI NOV 20 13:30 EST	1074.2	LOSS

On Monday, November 16, 2015, an alert was generated for two end-of-week binary trades on the Nadex platform: it was a bet that gold would decline by the end of the week (Table 7.2). It was not technical analysis that was predominant, but sentiment analysis. The first trade was a deep-in-the-money sell order that gold would not be above 1104.5. The second trade was an out-of-the-money order that gold would go below 1074. Gold settled at 1074.2, close for the out-of-money play but not enough.

The Greek Crisis

The Eurozone, with its single currency, means the EUR/USD continues to generate a perennial source of uncertainty and volatility. The fact is that it is tough to sustain economic growth in countries that have huge public sector welfare states. With the globalization of the world economy, countries with large public sectors will find it more difficult than ever to compete. In recent years, particularly since the financial credit crunch of 2008, the financial stability of countries such as Ireland, Greece, Spain, and Italy have been a focus of the markets. The bond markets and the currency markets reflect these concerns. We can see how much a higher yield the Greek two-year bond had to offer above the benchmark German two-year bond (Figure 7.8). This was in response to the downgraded confidence in Greece by the bond market to meet its fiscal requirements. In any case, for the binary option trader, the EUR/USD provides a trading opportunity when news hits the headlines about financial crisis. This happened in May when Greece's debt problem surfaced again. The rumors of a Greek pullout of the euro were all over the Net. The EUR/USD weakened. Given these rumors and market reactions, the binary option trading strategy could be, of course, to follow the mood of the market and bet the EUR/USD would continue to fall. The alternative, to bet the other way, may seem risky, but it felt correct because it's politically naïve to think that the Eurozone would let the Greek problem destroy it. Using this reasoning, and being a bit contrarian that the bad news was already out and the EUR/USD would actually go up, the following trade alert, on Thursday, May 26, 2011, was released. Notice this was a Thursday trade, with only one more day to expiration (see Figure 7.10).

The binary option trading alert written on this day was:

Bonus Binary Alert: Potential 15 Percent in Two Days
    The Greek crisis in Europe has pushed the EUR/USD through an important resistance. It's wavering though, and this gives us a bonus trade opportunity. It's an example of a deep-in-the money strategy. We are going with the sentiment that by Friday 3 P.M., the EUR/USD will stay above 1.4075.

FIGURE 7.10   EUR/USD Price Action May 20 to May 26, 2011

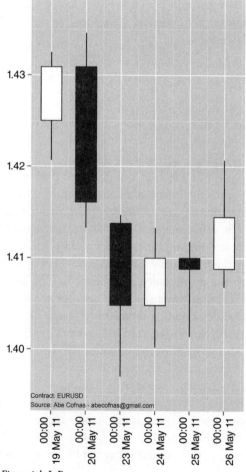

Source: Bloomberg Financial, L.P.

Trade Action to Take: Buy a Nadex weekly EUR/USD 1.4075 binary for under $90.

This costs us $80 to $89, and there is no guarantee. But if we're right, it will pay off $100, which gives us the 10 to 20 percent return.

The result of the trade alert was a 20 percent return in two days.

The bearish sentiment that seemed dominant early in the week on the EUR/USD because of the Greek situation, did not last and the EUR/USD broke through resistance. Therefore, buying a binary on the euro to expire higher than 1.4075 trade can be considered as a contrarian bounce of support; a deep-in-the-money trade playing on the bearish sentiment being an emotional panic in the midst of the Greek default fear.

The Greek debt problem seems to be a gift that keeps giving trading opportunities. The concern about a Greek debt default built up to a new crisis level as the Greek parliament scheduled a June 29 critical vote on a severe austerity program to meet the demands of the European Central Bank to provide further aid to Greece. The markets were nervous. Headlines alerted readers to the upcoming suicide votes for the Greek parliament because a no vote was considered a catastrophic event. This actually set up a trading opportunity in the DAX 30 (Figure 7.11). Here is what the Agora alert said on the morning of Monday, June 27 at 10:15 A.M.:

The 7225 binary is being offered at $35, making it an out-of-the-money play—not too deep but worthwhile. If it works, it provides us a nearly 3:1 return.

Trade Action to Take: Buy two or more Nadex weekly Germany 30 7225 binaries at market.

FIGURE 7.11 DAX 30 Reacts to Greek Crisis Week of June 27

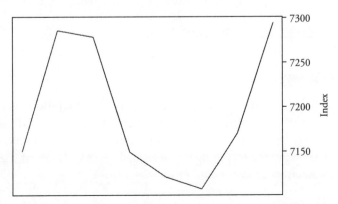

The Greek parliament approved the austerity package on June 29 and the DAX 7225 binary moved in-the-money, providing a 3:1 return for those who held the position to expiration on Friday, July 1.

The market conditions around the Greek crisis showed that the market pricing on binaries that are out-of-the-money, are often mispriced, reflecting extremes in pessimism.

Crude Oil and Near-the-Money Strategy

The oil complex is another underlying market that almost weekly presents the opportunity to use different binary trading strategies. In late January, revolts in Tunisia and Egypt erupted and raised the level of volatility in oil. In fact, oil prices surged from below $85 to near $100 from January 1 to March 1, 2011 (Figure 7.12). By Tuesday, February 1, 2011, at 2:15 P.M., the crude oil market was moving fast due to the fast-moving news from Cairo (Figure 7.13). The conditions were ripe for an at-the-money binary option trade. Notice that the cost of buying was at $45. Here is the real-time recommendation that was released.

The Agora alert on this day was:

> Action Alert: Take 38 Percent Profits Now!
>
> Yesterday, I recommended two oil binary plays as a way to cash in on uncertainty in Egypt. Now, with word that Egyptian President Mubarak won't run again, there might be some calm in the markets. So we're going to jump out of our more speculative of the binary plays.
>
> Action to Take: Sell all of your Nadex weekly crude oil 89.75 binary options.
>
> They're currently at $62—representing a 38 percent gain from our $45 entry price. Not bad at all!
>
> And we'll continue to hold the 87.75 oil binaries for now.

The result was a quick 38 percent win!

ATM Bounce Strategy

What can we learn from the oil trades during the Egyptian turmoil?

Essentially, if the underlying market patterns look like they are about to break out, the best strategy that fits this condition is an at-the-money or near-the-money strategy. The reasoning is that a small move will convert the binary contract to result in an in-the-money settlement.

FIGURE 7.12   West Texas Oil from January 1 to March 1, 2011

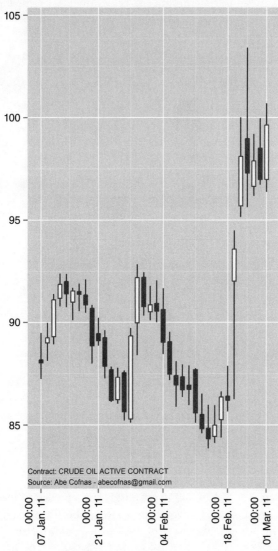

Another version of an at-the-money bounce strategy would be to play bounces off either side. Bounce plays are in the lingo of technical analysis: *mean reversion* plays betting that the price will move back toward the middle of the range. The challenge for the bounce strategy is to decide how far it will bounce off support or resistance and how quickly it will do that. A good method for a bounce trade is not to go to expiration but to select a target price to close the position. At-the-money bounce trades, costing $45 to $55 to get in, would

FIGURE 7.13   West Texas Oil During Week of January 30 to February 5, 2011

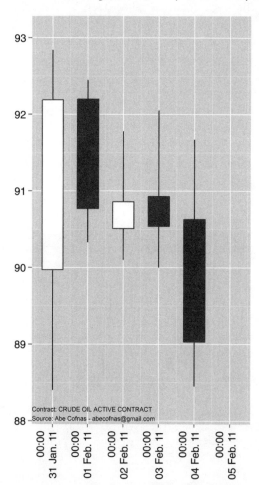

receive an objective of $75 to $80 to get out. Using a predetermined close order, the return in these conditions would be a respectable 77 percent. This can be within hours or just a few days. An alternative version of the at-the-money bounce play would be when the binary option strike price is in the middle of the range between support and resistance. In this scenario, the trader is really riding the natural oscillation of the price action. I call this vibrating your way to profits.

Breakout Plays

Markets break out when you least expect it. When this happens, the binary option trader can use technical analysis to trade the reaction. However, there are predictive patterns that are preludes to breaking out. Such patterns are observed when the price forms narrow sideways channels, triangles, and wedges. In these conditions, bullish and bearish sentiment is in a tug of war, resulting in a tight range. Markets, by their very nature, abhor a vacuum of information. As a result, the sideways pattern can be considered the calm before, or in fact after, the storm. Such patterns calibrate well with putting on a binary option breakout strategy.

Once a sideways or cluster of market pauses is detected, the challenge to the trader is to anticipate which side the breakout will occur. Will it be a breakout of support or resistance? One of the early tasks for putting on a breakout trade is to locate resistance and support and find the binary contract just above it to allow the benefit of a big market move. If the trader cannot make a conclusive determination of the direction of the breakout, a straddle play can also be applied, which plays a breakout in either direction. Breakout plays are most commonly connected to economic data releases or reactions to key statements by central bankers. For example, the statements of the Federal Open Market Committee and the statements of key central bankers, such as Trichet's on May 5, provided ideal conditions for trading breakout plays. The statement was scheduled, so traders could expect some movement. Trichet surprised the market with dovish comments about intended interest rate increases. The result was a selloff of the EUR/USD (Figure 7.14). Breakout plays are most appropriate on economic data releases.

FIGURE 7.14 EUR/USD Sells Off in Reaction to Trichet Remarks

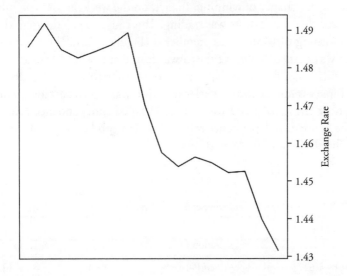

An interesting signal to the trader to play the breakout pattern is one that is most ignored. It is actually the previous failed breakout trade on the same underlying market. Traders often will encounter a sequence of losses and then give up. But this kind of reasoning can be counterproductive. Sometimes the trader is timing the breakout too early. In fact, if the previous week's breakout trade failed, the probability that the next one will work is actually greater because markets don't stay sideways too long. The following is an example of a breakout trade alert that worked out that was based on locating a sideways channel on the GBP/USD.

The Scottish Independence Referendum and the GBP/USD

In the fall of September 2014, the attention of world markets, and particularly the British pound, centered on the upcoming vote on Scottish independence. On September 18, 2014, the Scottish independence referendum was scheduled and the election would decide if Scotland would become an independent country. Obviously, the outcome would be important to the economy of Great Britain and would affect its currency, the British pound. The weeks leading up to the referendum generated great anxiety and intensity. Political polling started to influence markets and in the summer of 2014, the GBP/USD was beginning to reflect anxiety and optimism about the outcome of the referendum. A yes vote was feared and the GBP/USD began to decline in value (Figure 7.15). As August ended, the GBP/USD had actually begun to rise. But, in September, popular opinion started to show that the yes vote had a great chance of winning. In fact, on the weekend of September 7, a poll showed that the yes vote was leading. This caused a gap down in the GBP on the morning of Monday, September 8 (Figure 7.16). The binary play in this case was that such a move down was fear, but it would take a few weeks for the polls to confirm that the fear was over. Therefore, a selling deep in the money binary trade for end of week expiration was a correct trade (Table 7.3). Notice how the GBP/USD rose after the failed independence referendum vote. The Scottish Independence referendum is a good example of why binary traders should look to trade elections.

TABLE 7.3 Binary Option Trade on Scottish Independence Vote

Underlying Market/ Contract	Expiration Date	Bid	Direction of Trade
GBP/USD > 1.6275	12-SEP-14	17.3	SELL

FIGURE 7.15 GBP/USD Stable in August 2014 Reflecting Expectations of a No Vote on Independence

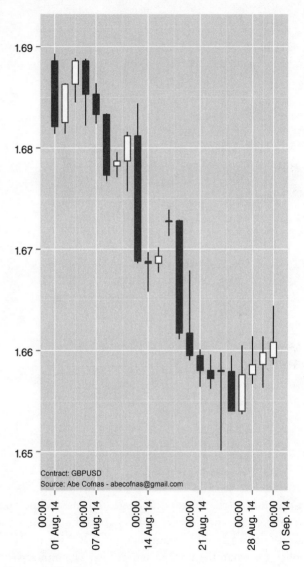

In It to Win It: The DOOM Strategy

Let's consider the DOOM trade. This refers to *deep-out-of-the-money* plays. In DOOM, the trader assumes that at any week, markets can go crazy, and therefore puts on several DOOM plays. They may not always work out, but when markets experience selloffs, those putting on binary option

FIGURE 7.16   GBP/USD Selloff in Fear of Scottish Independence Vote

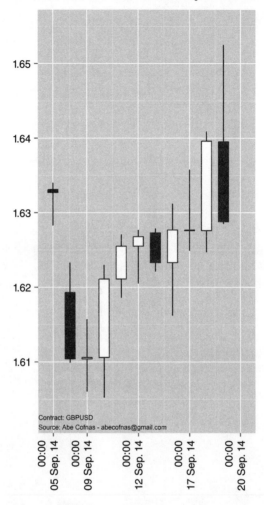

deep-out-of-the-money trades get the huge returns. While most trading occurs when markets are in relatively normal conditions, when major selloffs do not occur, it's not a bad idea to put on one DOOM play each week as an insurance policy for when the unexpected occurs. The only caveat with such an approach is it will not pay off all the time.

During the week ending July 1, 2014, however, almost every DOOM strategy on indexes did pay off. The pessimism and fear over the Greek crisis, plus the nervousness of the market in relationship to U.S. debt negotiations, created a very low price on the S&P 500 out-of-the-money ladders. Here is what the Agora binary alert stated on Monday, June 27, at 10:15 A.M.

Finally, the federal debt ceiling negotiations set up the DOOM play of the week. The situation between Congress and the president is very tenuous. Any sign that a compromise is coming will cheer the markets, but if there is still a deadlock going into the July Fourth holiday, we can expect a big selloff. This possibility leads to the following deep-out-of-the-money trade on the S&P 500:

Trade Action: Buy two or more Nadex weekly U.S. 500 1296.5 binaries at market.

With the S&P 500 Sept. futures—the binaries' underlying instrument—at 1268, a DOOM binary at 1296.5 at $15.50 provides a greater than 6:1 return.

With the Greek parliament approval of the austerity plan, the markets moved strongly into the money for a very large return on the DOOM play as the S&P 500 overnight doubled the binary option offer price and actually went in-the-money, returning $100 for every $15.50 lot [Figure 7.17].

FIGURE 7.17   S&P 500 Soars in Response to Greek Vote

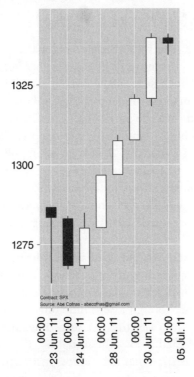

When Markets Are Overextended: Selling the Ladders

There are times when markets have extended beyond expectations into outlier statistical territory. These are situations in which new highs or lows have been created at a very fast pace. Taking a contrarian position in these conditions means anticipating that the crowd is wrong, exhausted, or that a natural retracement is bound to happen. The strategy to be employed in this scenario is selling the extreme ladders. Using the bid/ask range as a criterion, binary contracts that are $10 to $15 or less are essentially targets of contrarian thinking. Selling the binary bid would mean paying $100 bid price. A $15 ask price would reflect mean that the traders are assigning only a 15 percent probability of success. The seller would, at best, keep the $10. Before one employs this strategy, the question becomes: Is it worth it? Selling premium seems, at first glance, to provide easy pickings for the trader. However, it can be a very dangerous strategy. We need to remember that underlying markets that are extended become extended for a fundamental reason. Unless there is evidence of a change in the fundamentals, playing a reversal of an extended trend is fraught with danger.

Surprise Event Risks: The Great 2011 Japanese Earthquake

We have seen markets riled by surprise events. Earthquakes and revolts and terrorist attacks have in common, at first, the element of surprise. Initial news shocks the markets. But these events also have in common surprise followed by the reaction of the markets similar to a chemical reaction diffusion process. The markets react and then the initial shock wave is diffused out. It is in the reaction phase when binary option trading opportunities occur. The great Japanese earthquake of March 11, 2011 is a case in point.

Let's look at what happened in reaction to the Japanese earthquake of March 11. The Japanese earthquake immediately brought USD/JPY currency pair into play. The initial reaction of the yen was to strengthen. The morning before the earthquake, the USD/JPY pair was at 82. It descended to 76.25 by March 17 in reaction to the devastation (Figure 7.18A). This 7 percent decline in the currency pair was a surprise to many traders, as such a surprising strengthening of the currency is anathema to an economy in shock. But the crowd reacted to rumors of repatriation. This is when Japanese companies sell foreign assets and convert the cash to yen to balance their books. In any case, the yen surged against the U.S. dollar. In response to the Japan earthquake, the initial reaction was also a decline in the Nikkei (Figure 7.18B). What is also most instructive is the relationship

FIGURE 7.18A USD/JPY Dives 7 Percent in Reaction to Earthquake

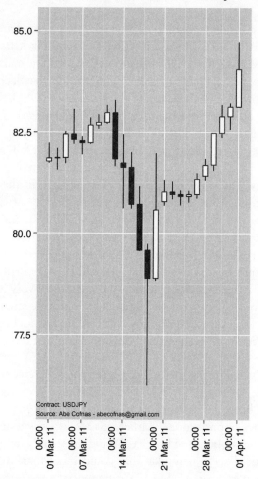

FIGURE 7.18B Nikkei and S&P 500 Co-Movement in Reaction to Earthquake

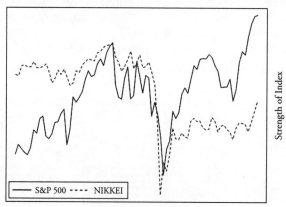

between the Nikkei and the S&P 500. As we can see, they moved in tandem (Figure 7.18B).

Other global fundamental forces were triggered immediately. The totally unpredictable earthquake caused a reaction in the oil markets. Oil fell as the market perceived a disruption in demand coming from a major global economy such as Japan. This reaction was in anticipation that Japanese refineries were shutting down. But let's get to the real sizzler—the USD/JPY movements that became the object of an extraordinary binary play (Figure 7.18A). Keep in mind that the chart of the USD/JPY is the dollar versus the yen. So a strong yen will have the chart going in a down direction as the dollar falls against the yen.

One of the features associated with trading currency pairs also benefited the strategy. The USD/JPY can be traded at night in the United States. The 12-hour difference in time allows an evening trade. After a very strong strengthening of the yen, the opportunity for buying an out-of-the-money binary option contract on the yen was irresistible. Watching the reports that weekend from Japan was riveting. It took a lot of patience not to trade on Monday morning, but on Wednesday, March 16 at 6:50 P.M., the Nadex weekly USD/JPY binary strike price of 79.25 reached a very low ask price of $22. Hours before, the spot market actually hit a historic strength of the yen, near 76.00. It was a classic case of a huge outlier, black swan event! In the *Strategic Currency Trader* newsletter, the following recommendation was issued:

> Bonus Alert: Following the Bouncing Yen for 400 Percent Return in Three Days
>
> It has been an extraordinary week that has generated some extraordinary opportunities. Earlier this week, I suggested two yen binary plays, hoping for a bounce. While those are a long way from panning out, I see a new play that could more than make up for them. As you know, the USD/JPY experienced a historic downward spike due to the unfolding disasters in Japan. But the Bank of Japan is not likely to let the yen stay at historical strength. So we have a limited window to try to catch a bounce.
>
> Trade Action to Take: Buy a weekly Nadex USD/JPY 79.25 binary for $25 or better.

The result was a successful in-the-money settlement by Friday returning 4:1! When surprises hit the global markets, the best conditions emerge for out-of-the-money and deep-out-of-the-money strategies.

THE TANKAN REPORT

For traders looking to trade the USD/JPY binary options it's very important to know when the Tankan report comes out. The survey is conducted to provide an accurate picture of business trends of enterprises in Japan, thereby contributing to the appropriate implementation of monetary policy. The survey is conducted quarterly in March, June, September, and December. The survey results are released at the beginning of April, July, October, and mid-December (released at 8:50 A.M. Japanese Standard Time).

Chinese Yuan Devaluation, Shanghai Selloff and Binaries

Now, let's jump forward to one of the most important trading events in recent times. On August 11, 2015, the Chinese authorities devalued the yuan and the surprise action disrupted the global markets. The yuan was trading previously in a 2 percent volatility band. The move suddenly departed from that band. The reason for the devaluation was essentially to weaken the currency to stimulate exports, which had fallen over 8.3 percent from the previous year. But the devaluation created a signal that the world should be worried about China's growth. The Shanghai index and then the global markets subsequently sold off after this period, resulting in "black" Monday on August 24 (Figure 7.19). After the sell-off, the Chinese authorities intervened in their markets and stabilized the down trend.

A binary trading opportunity became irresistible when President Xi visited the United States during the week ending Sept 25. The China a50 weekly binary tracks the Shanghai index. Betting that during the week the president of China visits the United States, the market would NOT sell off was a classic sentiment play. The exact alert was to: BUY CHINA A50 9425 STRIKE PRICE @ ASK 57.75 (Table 7.4).

The winning trade returned $100 fixed payout and as a result the profit was 42.25, generating a return of 73 percent on the initial risk of $597.75. This was an example of when sentiment analysis and an understanding of geopolitics generated the rationale for a deep-in-the-money position that had a strong chance of winning.

FIGURE 7.19   Shanghai Selloff on Black Monday

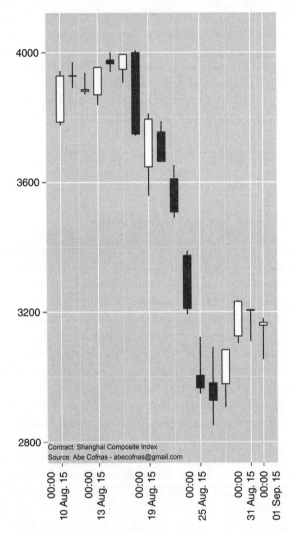

Russia Invades Ukraine

The crisis in Ukraine in March of 2014 provides another example of how markets react and counter-react in a sudden event crisis. Once again, the USD/JPY reaction to the Ukraine crisis was a classic case of risk aversion on Monday to risk appetite by Friday (Figure 7.20).

The lesson learned from this response is for traders to look at doing a contrarian binary trade when a sudden event causes markets to sell off. The end-of-week duration is the best one to use.

TABLE 7.4 China A50 Weekly Binary Trade

Binary Contract	Expiration	Trade Time	Trade	Price
China 50 (Oct) > 9425	25-SEP-15	9-22-00:13	BUY	57.75

FIGURE 7.20 USD/JPY Reaction to Ukraine Crisis: From Risk Aversion on Monday to Risk Appetite by Friday

Perfect Storm Conditions: U.S. Election Week

It's a good idea to trade binary options before a key election contest such congressional and the U.S. presidential votes. The quadrennial presidential election week is likely to result in extraordinary binary trading opportunities, especially if it is a closely predicted election. The good news is that we don't have to predict the winner. We just need to ride the volatility. It will not only be election week, but the ramp up to it, right after the September Labor Day holiday, is the traditional start of campaigning.

To best prepare for trading during an election week, it is very instructive to look at what happened in the important 2010 congressional elections. The 2010 U.S. congressional elections is a case study of known-in-advance conditions for large market reactions.

The week of November 1 had a confluence of three events: the U.S. elections on November 2, the Federal Open Market Committee (FOMC) statement on Wednesday at 2:15 P.M. regarding QE2 policy, and the non-farm payroll data release. There was more—on top of this trifecta of events were scheduled statements from the Bank of England, the European Central Bank, and the Bank of Japan. It was a combination that simulated an asteroid penetration of the atmosphere. The result was guaranteed price movements.

Here is an example of real-time analysis in the Agora report of this upcoming week and the resulting binary option strategy suggested.

Election Week Recommendations, Part 1
U.S. Election & FOMC Binary Plays
This week, the FOMC is expected to announce the start of its second round of quantitative easing, being called QE2. This combined with the election results will energize sentiment regarding the U.S. dollar. Even though the prevailing sentiment is bearish, there can be a large move in either direction. So we'll use USD/CHF binaries to capture any breakout moves in either direction. The U.S. dollar/Swiss franc (USD/CHF) is a great surrogate for U.S. dollar sentiment, as you can see in [Figure 7.21].

Trade Action to Take: Sell one or more Nadex weekly USD/CHF .9775 binaries.

Then buy one or more Nadex weekly USD/CHF 1.0075 binaries. With multiple binaries, you can leg out of positions during the part of a position to let the others ride.

At the time of the recommendation on Monday morning of election week, traders saw a sideways market in the USD/CHF. The USD/CHF was hovering above support. It looked like perfect conditions for a breakout pattern (Figure 7.22). Also, the binary option strike ladders for Monday morning

FIGURE 7.21   USD/CHF and U.S. Dollar Index

FIGURE 7.22 USD/CHF Sideways Pattern

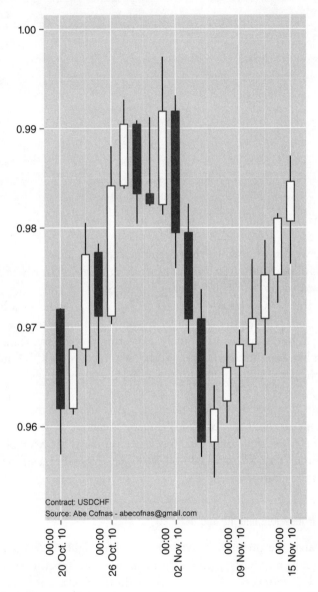

showed that the out-of-the-money strike prices were very cheap (Table 7.5). The spot price was around .9850.

Of course, the election week meant opportunities in the S&P 500. The S&P 500 was also noted to be in a sideways range on November 1, 2010 (Figure 7.23).

TABLE 7.5 Nadex Binary Option Strike Prices November 1 (November 5 Expiration Date)

Market	Bid ($)	Offer ($)
USD/CHF > 1.0175 (3 P.M.)	4	9
USD/CHF > 1.0075 (3 P.M.)	16	21.5
USD/CHF > 0.9975 (3 P.M.)	37	44
USD/CHF > 0.9775 (3 P.M.)	62.5	69
USD/CHF > 0.9975 (3 P.M.)	83	88
USD/CHF > 1.0075 (3 P.M.)	93.5	98
USD/CHF > 1.0175 (3 P.M.)	96	Not Shown

Here is what I said in the Agora *Strategic Currency Trader* alert:

While we don't know which way the market will move, the reward-to-risk opportunity is in a move up from current levels. My inclination was to try an 1180.5 binary, but at $60, the premium is too high. The 1200.5 binary is priced at $31 and provides us a better return, but will require a stronger move. Still, I am recommending taking a shot at the 1200.5 binary, expecting positive market action after a big Republican victory and the first injection of QE2. It pays off if the S&P 500 is above 1200.5 at 4:15 P.M. on Friday.

This election week produced phenomenal results. The markets followed this script perfectly. The USD/CHF binary breakout play paid off with a return of $100 per share on a total $40 cost. Similarly, the S&P 500 1200.5 binary contract cost $32 and paid off $100 per share after a strong move in reaction to the election (Table 7.6).

Correlation Trades: Running the Board

We know that the underlying markets are often highly correlated, or have strong co-movements, as global sentiment on risk appetite or risk aversion cascades around the world. Many of these correlations were reviewed throughout this book. The trader should be aware of the correlations because they lead to correlation trades, or running the board. One approach to applying this strategy is to trade two or more different underlying binary markets that are highly correlated to each other. The rationale is that being right on one pair allows one to increase the return by putting on a trade in the

FIGURE 7.23 S&P in Sideways Range before November 2010 Elections

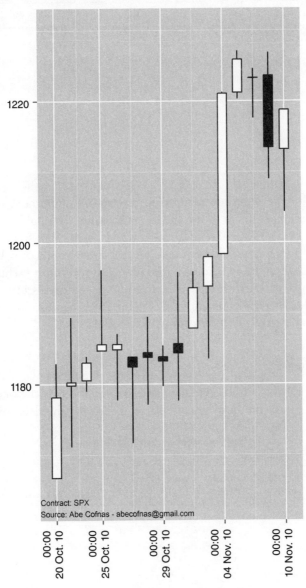

correlated markets. Crude oil and Canadian dollar, USD/JPY, and S&P 500, AUD/USD, and copper are proven strongly correlated pairs. The correlations may not be the same strength at any given time. When they reach above 70 percent, however, the conditions are good for correlated trading. Table 7.7 shows recent correlation data between these pairs.

TABLE 7.6 S&P 500 Election Week Ladders (November 5 Expiration Date)

Market (4:15 P.M.)	Bid	Offer
US500 (DEC) > 1240.5	1	5.5
US500 (DEC) > 1220.5	10.5	15.5
US500 (DEC) > 1200.5	32.5	38.5
US500 (DEC) > 1180.5	62	68
US500 (DEC) > 1160.5	85	90
US500 (DEC) > 1140.5	95	99.5
US500 (DEC) > 1120.5	96	N/A

Accessing the latest information on correlation is important, and an easy way to accomplish this is to use the free correlation data published at www .mrci.com/special/corr030.php. This site tracks correlations from 30 days to 180 days. The trader should keep in mind that correlation data will vary over time and tracking the correlations from time to time is most useful.

Trading binaries with one-week and intraday periods can be aided by scanning shorter-term correlations. A site for accessing shorter-term correlations is: www.myfxbook.com/forex-market/correlation.

Noncorrelated Trades

The other side of a correlated trading strategy is to diversify the week's binary trades along with the most noncorrelated. Following the data presented in

TABLE 7.7 Sample 30-Day Correlations between Underlying Equity Markets from January 2010 to January 2011

EUR/USD	FTSE 100	Germany 100	India 50	Japan 225	Korea 200	US 500	U.S. Tech 100	Wall St. 30
FTSE 100	1							
Germany 100	0.77	1						
India 50	0.68	0.86	1					
Japan 225	0.37	−0.38	−0.32	1				
Korea 200	0.75	0.95	0.90	−0.09	1			
US500	0.95	0.83	0.65	0.42	0.79	1		
U.S. Tech 100	0.89	0.93	0.81	0.16	0.90	0.95	1	
Wall St. 30	0.95	0.87	0.74	0.30	0.84	0.98	0.97	1

Table 7.7, a trader looking to have minimum correlations in trading underlying equity indexes would be trading the Japan 225 and the FTSE 100, which show the lowest correlation of 37 percent.

Combination Strategies

The review of binary option trading strategies essentially implies a pure approach—putting on one strategy at a time. In fact, this is rarely recommended. The alternatives to pure strategies are combination strategies that look to benefit from a variety of market conditions during a week. What should be considered is a mixed set of strategies. For example, putting on three deep-in-the-money trades with one deep-out-of-the-money trade. Alternatively, the trader could be putting on three deep-out-of-the-money, three deep-in-the-money, and four at-the-money trades. Regardless of the combination, option strategies should match market conditions. Two combined strategy examples are:

1. Put on: three deep-in-the-money with one deep-out-of-the-money.
2. Put on: one-third deep-out-of-the-money, one-third deep-in-the-money, and one-third at-the-money.

There are many different strategies to match a variety of market conditions and technical patterns. It's a good idea to try all of them over time to build your skills (Figure 7.24).

This chapter has provided a tour of how binary option trading strategies are intimately related to understanding not only the technical conditions of the market, but the fundamentals and the prevailing sentiment moods.

Selecting the Right Underlying Market: Leaderboard Selection Strategies

Beyond being able to scan market patterns and follow news events, trading binaries comes down to selecting the right underlying market to trade. Many traders have a tendency to trade what they like, rather than spend time scanning the global markets. The disadvantage of trading what one likes lies in the potential of missing other profitable opportunities. A remedy to this myopic tendency is implementing a Leaderboard Selection Strategy.

FIGURE 7.24   Market Conditions and Binary Option Trading Strategies

Market Condition	Strength	Binary Strategy
Trending	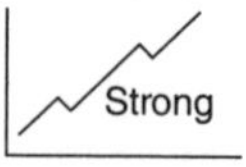 Strong	Buy Deep-in-the-Money
	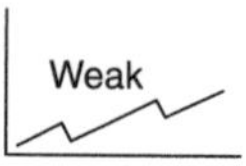 Weak	Buy or Sell At-the-Money
	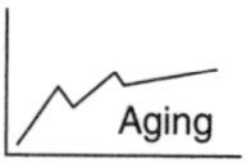 Aging	Sell Out-of-the-Money
Parabolic	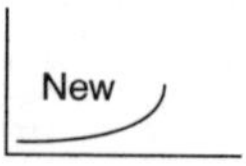 New	Buy At-the-Money
	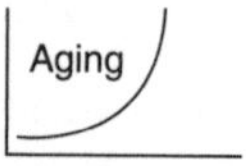 Aging	Sell At-the-Money Sell Out-of-the-Money
Sideways	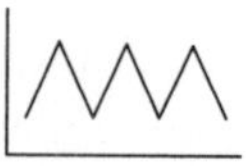	Sell Strangle

KEY QUESTIONS EACH WEEK FOR EVERY BINARY TRADER

PART 1, FUNDAMENTAL ANALYSIS

Here are some key questions that should be on your checklist before you take off on your binary trade.

- Which markets are the big movers?
- Which markets are on top of the leaderboard?
- Which markets are at the bottom?
- Is the market "risk-on" or "risk-off"?
- Where is gold and what does it mean for market direction?
- Is the U.S. dollar sentiment bullish or bearish?
- Is crude oil up or down?
- Is gold in a range or breaking up or down?

- Is China's economy expected to increase in GDP?
- Which markets are diverging from their usual correlations?
- What is the "balance of fears" facing the markets as the week begins?
- Did you check this week's "economic calendar"?
- Is there a special economic data release announcement coming in the week that will move the markets?
- Are there elections in the coming weeks that are likely to affect the market?
- Are interest rates expected to go up or down at the next Central Bank decision?
- Which central banks are considering increases in rates?

The leaderboard selection strategy answers the question of which markets are the big movers? A good way to choose what to trade is to trade what the markets are paying attention to.

A heat map is a great tool for this (Table 7.8). At any moment in time during the week, some markets are outperforming others. In other words, some are hot and some are not. A good idea is to select the best performer and the worst performer as targets for your trades. A useful Internet site for finding the latest movers in the market is www.finviz.com. It provides what is known as a "heat map" of price movements. This is a quick way of spotting the big movers in either direction. In the heat map that follows, the JPY and the CAD are the biggest winner and loser in terms of relative performance. The binary trader would, using this leaderboard, look for trading opportunities in these two underlying markets.

TABLE 7.8 One-Day Relative Performance Sample Heat Map

Percentage Gain in Price					
2.00	JPY				
1.50					
1.0					
0.52	AUD				
0.47		CHF			
0.37			EUR		
−0.06				GBP	
−0.16					CAD

Another site, www.myfxbook.com/forex-market/heat-map, generates rankings in pips, or in percent against a range of time durations (1 minute, 5 minutes, 15 minutes, 30 minutes, 1 hour, 4 hours, daily, weekly, and monthly).

Relative changes in which markets move greatest in either direction generates strategies to follow or fade a particular market.

References

Cofnas, Abe. 2011. "Action Alert: Playing Market Fears for a Chance at 72 Percent Gains or More." *Agora Financial* (April 18). http://strategiccurrencytrader.agorafinancial.com/2011/04/18/action-alert-playing-market-fears-for-a-chance-at-72-gains-or-more/.

Cofnas, Abe. 2011. "Bonus Binary Alert: Potential 15 Percent in Two Days," *Agora Financial* (May 26). http://strategiccurrencytrader.agorafinancial.com/2011/05/26/bonus-binary-alert-potential-15-in-two-days/.

Cofnas, Abe. 2011. "Action Alert: Take 38 Percent Profits Now!" *Agora Financial* (February 1). http://strategiccurrencytrader.agorafinancial.com/2011/02/01/action-alert-take-38-profits-now/.

Nazareth, Rita, Cordell Eddings, and Inyoung Hwang. 2011. "Stocks Sink on U.S. Credit Outlook as Euro Falls on Debt Crises." Bloomberg.com (April 18).

CHAPTER 8

Analyzing NFP Data for Binary Trading

This chapter provides strategies for evaluating and trading the nonfarm payroll data release. The NFP report is considered the key economic data release in the world. The United States Department of Labor releases the NFP report on the first Friday of every month at 8:30 A.M. EST. All traders are watching and markets are affected by it as it signals a monthly gauge on the strength of the U.S. economy, this data release and the binary option related to it is one of the most important offered to traders. It is also one of the most challenging. The opportunity to trade the NFP data release is offered by Nadex and by IG, as there are specific binary ladders on this release (Table 8.1). Unlike binaries that have an actual underlying market such as a currency or commodity, the NFP binaries have job levels as the underlying market.

Another related event risk binary offered is on the jobless claims data. The jobless claims underlying market is simply the economic data record that is reported on the number of first-time claims for U.S. unemployment benefits. These are applications for jobless benefits. While important, it is not as important as the NFP report. Traders should become competent in trading binaries relating to the NFP release before they start trading the jobless claims data.

Trading the binary options on event data releases presents a unique set of challenges to the trader as well as the market maker. The trader faces the challenge of how to conduct technical analysis of the jobless claims and nonfarm payroll charts. The answers to these questions are not obvious or easy. The uncertainty around the data releases of jobless claims and nonfarm payroll charts should not be surprising. There are frequent surprises in the numbers.

163

TABLE 8.1   NFP Binary Option Ladder For NFP Data Release February 5, 2016

Nonfarm Payroll > 260,000	EXPIRATION DATE FEB 5 8:30 A.M. EST	BID/ASK 12/22
Nonfarm Payroll > 230,000	EXPIRATION DATE FEB 5 8:30 A.M. EST	BID/ASK 25/35
Nonfarm Payroll > 200,000	EXPIRATION DATE FEB 5 8:30 A.M. EST	BID/ASK 40/50
Nonfarm Payroll > 170,000	EXPIRATION DATE FEB 5 8:30 A.M. EST	BID/ASK 70/80
Nonfarm Payroll > 140,000	EXPIRATION DATE FEB 5 8:30 A.M. EST	BID/ASK 85/95

Headlines following the jobless claims data releases reflect the ongoing surprise of the results. On April 28, 2011, a Bloomberg headline was "Jobless Claims in U.S. Unexpectedly Rise to Three Month High." Another headline on May 5, 2011: "Jobless Claims in U.S. Unexpectedly Jump on One-Time Events." What is a typical reaction to surprise? A major surprise happened on the October 2015 NFP data release on November 4. The nonfarm payroll report astounded the market with results of 271,000 new jobs. This result signaled a strengthening U.S. economy and increased market confidence that interest rates would be raised by the end of 2015. One can also note the decline in the NFP results prior to the 2008 collapse (Figure 8.1).

Evidently, our best number crunchers don't know how to accurately predict these economic levels. The question arises, why should the binary option trader have a better handle on the results? Certainly, the binary option trader will have a challenging time mastering trading binaries relating to predictions of employment levels. In any case, there are some useful approaches to deciding on direction of the NFP report. One strategy is to locate what the "gurus" are forecasting. There are several sources of professional forecasts. A good place to start is the latest professional economic forecasts of the Federal Reserve Bank of Philadelphia. It issues a quarterly *Survey of Professional Forecasters* (https://www.philadelphiafed.org/research-and-data/real-time-center/survey-of-professional-forecasters/). Here is what the last survey of 2015 stated:

> Growth in real GDP in 2016 and 2017 looks a little slower now than it did three months ago, according to 45 forecasters surveyed

FIGURE 8.1 NFP Results

by the Federal Reserve Bank of Philadelphia. The forecasters currently see growth in the annual-average level of real GDP at 2.6 percent in 2016 and 2.5 percent in 2017. These current estimates represent downward revisions to the outlook of three months ago, when the forecasters thought 2016 growth would be 2.8 percent and 2017 growth would be 2.6 percent. Notably, the forecasters have raised their growth estimates for 2018. They now see real GDP growing 2.8 percent in 2018, up from the previous estimate of 2.4 percent.

A slightly improved outlook for the unemployment rate accompanies the outlook for growth. The forecasters predict the unemployment rate will be an annual average of 5.3 percent in 2015, before falling to 4.8 percent in 2016, 4.7 percent in 2017, and 4.7 percent in 2018. The projections for 2016 and 2017 are below those of the last survey.

On the jobs front, the panelists have revised upward their estimates for job gains in the first three quarters of 2016. The forecasters see nonfarm payroll employment growing at a rate of 201,500 jobs per month this quarter and 188,200 jobs per month next quarter. The forecasters' projections for the annual-average level of nonfarm payroll employment suggest job gains at a monthly rate of 241,800 in 2015 and 197,000 in 2016. (These annual-average estimates are computed as the year-to-year change in the annual-average level of nonfarm payroll employment, converted to a monthly rate.)

In the Philadelphia survey, the trader can obtain very detailed summaries of different forecasts regarding real GDP, unemployment rate, payrolls, and inflation levels. (Federal Reserve Bank of Philadelphia 2015)

For those traders looking to gain an edge in predicting a strong NFP report, checking on several sources of economic forecasts is advisable. One of the most interesting is the *Anxious Index*. It reflects whether economists are hopeful or anxious about the prospects of GDP growth or decline and the prospects of a recession. It is taken every quarter by the Federal Reserve Bank of Philadelphia. They describe it: "The anxious index peaks during recessions, then declines when recovery seems near." It can be used by traders as a contrarian signal for the economy. It's a good idea to keep tabs on the results (see Figure 8.2). We can also see how the Anxious Index was at extreme highs before the financial collapse of 2008 (Figure 8.3).

To be sure, a great deal of quantitative research is being done to attempt to obtain better predictions for nonfarm payrolls. Recent research uses Google Trends as a predictive tool for these event binaries. Researchers D'Amuri and

FIGURE 8.2   Anxious Index Correlates Negatively with Recessions

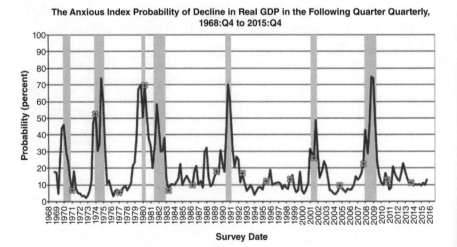

The Anxious Index Probability of Decline in Real GDP in the Following Quarter Quarterly, 1968:Q4 to 2015:Q4

FIGURE 8.3 Anxious Index and the Financial Collapse

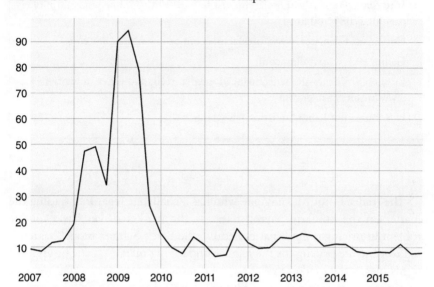

Marcucci from the Bank of Italy said about the use of Google to quantify search trends: "We suggest the use of an Internet job-search indicator (the Google Index, GI) as the best leading indicator to predict the U.S. unemployment rate. . . . We find that models augmented with the GI outperform the traditional ones in predicting the monthly unemployment rate, even in most state-level forecasts and in comparison with the survey of professional forecasters."

Look Online

The Conference Board's Index of Leading Economic Indicators: www.conference-board.org

Institute for Supply Management (ISM): www.ism.ws/

Survey of Professional Forecasters: www.phil.frb.org/econ/spf/index.html

The Anxious Index: www.phil.frb.org/files/spf/anxind.html

Wall Street Journal Economic Forecast Survey: http://online.wsj.com/public/page/0,,2_0891,00.html

Consensus Estimates: www.forexfactory.com or www.forexpros.com

Gallup Poll: www.gallup.com

Business Insider, a site with financial, media, tech, and other industry news: www.businessinsider.com

U.S. Bureau of Labor Statistics: www.bls.gov

The trader is not the only one who has a challenge regarding trading the binaries on the nonfarm payroll releases. The market maker has a unique problem in pricing event binaries because the Black-Scholes model, which is used to generate pricing for the regular underlying markets, can't be applied. So this means the market maker has a lot more risk exposure when deciding to put on a price for a particular binary ladder.

Key Steps Before Trading Nonfarm Payroll and Job Claims Binaries

There are several analytical questions that need to be asked and answered by anyone set on trading these event risks.

What Is the Consensus on the Coming Data Release?

Several analysts and economists offer their opinions about the upcoming numbers. Reuters and Bloomberg poll a sample of experts. Tradingeconomics .com releases estimates as well. Historically, there is surprise in actual versus estimate outcomes. Sometimes there is great surprise and as a result the markets react with volatility. However, those traders who want to develop an opinion of whether the nonfarm payroll will hit new highs or lows can get into the data at a more focused level. They can seek to answer several questions.

Is There a Trending Pattern in the Data?

The United States Department of Labor issues a report called the *Unemployment Insurance Weekly Claims Report*. The four-week moving average seasonally adjusted (SA) is the key row to look at.

Look at the data and ask yourself: Is the moving average of claims going up, down, or sideways? The trader can also apply basic technical analysis to the employment data. For example, on the NFP chart (Figure 8.1), one can apply classical trend line, support, and resistance analysis to the data and we can see that from January 2006 to April 2009, job losses were increasing every month, but stopped decreasing in April 2009. A binary trader would logically play the downtrend during this period by betting that the NFP report would not generate new highs. This would mean selling the highest or next to the highest ladder. Noticing that a shift in the trend occurred after April 2009, the binary strategy that would have been logical would have been to bet on an increasing ability to generate jobs, or that no new lows would occur. This would mean buying the lowest or next to the lowest binary ladder. When the NFP shows a sideways action, a wide binary option range trade would be logical.

Is There Consensus Error Bias?

Evaluating the technical trend can be supplemented by evaluating the trend in the consensus. Even more important is evaluating whether there is a bias in the consensus. Forecasts are often wrong, but more important to know is whether the error is underestimating or overestimating. In studying data produced by Tradingeconomics.com, we can see in Table 8.2 that there is a challenge in achieving accuracy.

TABLE 8.2 Actual versus Estimated Nonfarm Payroll Changes

Month	Consensus	Actual Results
Oct-2-2015	203k	142k
Nov-11-2015	180k	271k
Dec-4-2015	200k	211k

Here are some tips for traders of nonfarm payroll reports:

- If the most recent actual results were greater than the estimate, the strategy for the binary option trader for NFP data release is to go for out-of-the-money strike prices on the next release. Remember, since there is no underlying market, the consensus estimate can be used as the at-the-money spot market.
- If the recent actual results are below the consensus, the strategy for the binary option trader for the next data release is to go for playing in-the-money strike prices.
- If the employment data has no reliable trend, and is very choppy, find the strike price that is above but closest to the result, and the strike price that is below but closest to the results. Put on a breakout strategy.

- If NFP data breaks a trend line, use in-the-money or deep-in-the-money binary strike prices to go with the direction.
- If the jobless claims data breaks uptrend, or is getting close to breaking it, consider an out-of-the-money sell position.

Tactics for Trading NFP Report in Binaries

We have focused on analyzing the NFP data and getting a grip on direction. Let's focus on tactics. What are the alternative ways of trading the NFP report. This applies to any binary, whether it is a ladder binary or a regular high-low binary. There are several strategies.

First, it is important to note that one can trade the NFP report by trading binaries on the EUR/USD, USD/JPY, and the S&P 500. These markets will likely react and move big with the NFP results. The trader needs to choose an expiration that allows the trade to benefit from the momentum of the market. This means the expiration should be short-term from 1-minute to 30-minute durations. Regardless of the durations, there are several trading strategies to consider. Let's examine them now.

Strategy 1: Anticipate Data Release Results

In this strategy, the trader believes she knows what the results of the news release will be (see Figure 8.4 and Table 8.3). She consequently chooses a direction before the news release. If the trader was trading spot, the action would be to put on a

FIGURE 8.4   Anticipate Data Release Strategy

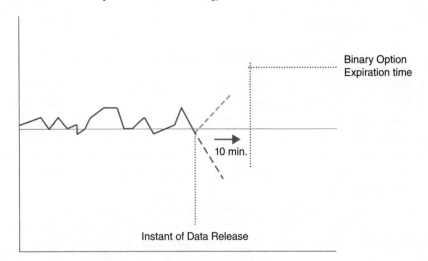

TABLE 8.3 Key Decisions on Strategy for Anticipating Data Release

Action	Advisory
Choose trade direction	Buy or sell
Choose option expiration	Select option that expires 5 to 10 minutes after data release
Execute trade	5 to 10 minutes before data release

market order before the news release in the anticipated direction. However, for binaries, the trader chooses an option that will expire shortly after the data release.

Strategy 2A: Trade at Data Release in a Bullish Direction

In this strategy, the market has reacted and it is going bullish (see Figure 8.5 and Table 8.4). The trade is to buy the next expiration binary, which will enable participation in the direction of the break. The disadvantage of this strategy is that prices could reverse and the reaction is not as strong to ride it out through the next expiration binary.

FIGURE 8.5 Bull Trading NFP at Data Release

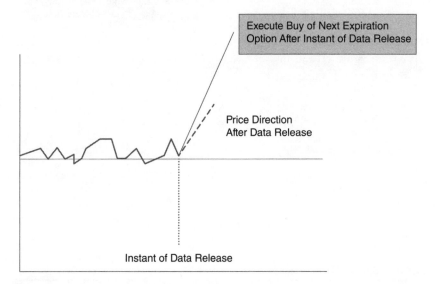

Execute Buy of Next Expiration Option After Instant of Data Release

Price Direction After Data Release

Instant of Data Release

TABLE 8.4 Key Decisions for Bull Trading NFP at Data Releases

Action	Advisory
Detect price direction at instant of data release	Choose buy if price direction is up
Select next expiration binary option	Execute next expiration binary option

Strategy 2B: Sell Trade at Data Release

The benefit of this strategy is that the trader doesn't have to guess the results of the news release (see Figure 8.6 and Table 8.5). The market has reacted and is bearish in this case. Go and sell the next expiration binary as soon as the news breaks out. It will enable participation in the direction of the break. The disadvantage of this strategy is that prices could reverse and the reaction is not as strong to ride it out through the next expiration binary.

Strategy 3A: (Buy) Trade at Fibonacci Points

In this strategy, the trader waits for the initial reaction of the news release to be over (see Figure 8.7 and Table 8.6). If the reaction is bullish, wait until the price starts reversing. The trader puts on a Fibonacci retracement tool and finds the key Fibonacci points. The trader waits for the market to go to those

FIGURE 8.6 Bear Trading NFP at Data Release

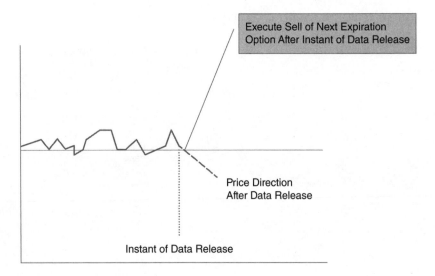

TABLE 8.5 Key Decisions for Bear Trading NFP at Data Release

Action	Advisory
Detect price direction at instant of data release	Choose sell if price direction is up
Select next expiration binary option	Execute next expiration binary option

FIGURE 8.7 Using Fibonacci Strategy for Buying after Data Release

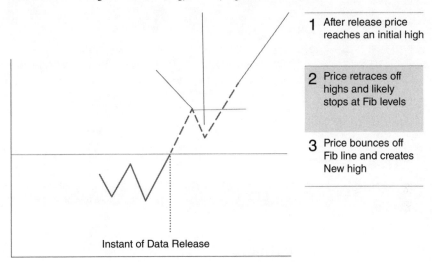

1 After release price reaches an initial high

2 Price retraces off highs and likely stops at Fib levels

3 Price bounces off Fib line and creates New high

Instant of Data Release

TABLE 8.6 Key Decision Steps for Bull Trading NPF Using Fibonacci Strategy

Action	Advisory
Wait for instant of data release	Detect buy direction of price upon data release
Wait for price to stop going up	Place a sell binary option (next-expiration) after price starts reversing back down
Wait for price to stop falling at likely Fib level	Place a buy binary option (next-expiration) as price resumes expiration as price resumes movement upward
Wait for price to break previous high	Place a binary option (next-expiration) as price breaks previous high

points and if the price resumes the initial direction up—put on the next expiration trade in the new direction.

Strategy 3B: (Sell) Trade at Fibonacci Points

In this strategy, the trader waits for the initial reaction of the news release, which in this scenario is a bearish reaction (see Figure 8.8 and Table 8.7). Wait for it to be over. The trader puts on a Fibonacci retracement tool and finds the key Fibonacci points. The trader waits for the market to go to those points. It will try to reverse back up. Put on a next expiration trade in the new direction.

FIGURE 8.8   Bear Trading NPF Using Fibonacci Strategy

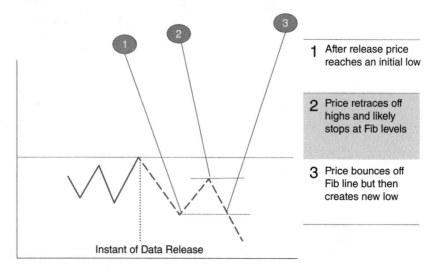

1   After release price
    reaches an initial low

2   Price retraces off
    highs and likely
    stops at Fib levels

3   Price bounces off
    Fib line but then
    creates new low

Instant of Data Release

TABLE 8.7   Key Decision Steps for Using Fibonacci Strategy for Trading NFP

Action	Advisory
Wait for instant of data release	Detect down direction of price upon data release
Wait for price to stop going down	Place a buy binary option (next-expiration) after price starts reversing back up
Wait for the price to stop retracing upward at likely Fib level	Place a sell binary option (next-expiration) as price resumes movement downward
Wait for price to break previous low	Place a buy binary option (next-expiration) as price breaks previous low

Timing and Managing Trades During the Week

We have considered event risks as triggered by political and market-driven events. But there is another kind of event risk—the days of the week. The process of analysis is important, but the probability of success also depends upon timing decisions. The trader has to learn which strategies work better on which days of the week.

Contrarian Mondays

Monday mornings (3 A.M. EST) are when the binary option trading week essentially begins. Monday mornings represent, perhaps, the best opportunity to be a contrarian. The distance in time from Monday morning when markets in Asia open to Friday afternoon when the U.S. equity markets close provides a great deal of room for the unexpected events and changes in the mood of the market. Abraham Lincoln referred to the silent artillery of time as one of the most powerful weapons. It is true for traders. Time fuels hope as well as delusion. The initial opinion polls that form around a binary option strike price on Monday morning are the most likely to change and be wrong. The market mood formed on Monday mornings is based on lagging information from the events of the previous week. The previous week's reaction to news and surprises has had time to diffuse. The new week presents new potential for mis-speculation and misjudgments. This leads to good conditions for putting on high return trades, offering more than 100 to 500 percent returns for the week. Monday morning becomes the best time slot for putting on initial trades.

Missing Monday: Initiating Trades on Tuesday

One strategy that requires some patience but can pay off strategically can be called Missing Monday. If Monday is the time when misjudgments occur, then Tuesday provides a reprieve. There may even be justification for waiting until Tuesday to do binary option trades. The rationale is that there is a value in waiting for more information. By Tuesday, initial assumptions about the week have been absorbed by the market, thereby offering less risk. Less risk, however, may mean lower returns. Putting on a trade on Tuesday offers less probable opportunities for 100 to 500 percent binary settlement values. Even so, on Tuesday, $30 to $45 ask prices still provide excellent return potential.

Surfing the Volatility Wave: At-the-Money Wednesdays

By Wednesday, the market has had time to absorb news. Price patterns have had time to solidify or probe their important levels of resistance and support. Emotions have dissipated somewhat and often what was expected on Monday morning has just collapsed and gone the other way. But by Wednesday, it is midweek in uncertainty. This makes Wednesday a good day for at-the-money (ATM) trades.

Going with the Crowd: Deep-in-the-Money Thursdays

Deep-in-the-money strategies make sense on Thursdays because, by that time, the market has formed a crowd or consensus of opinion on many of the market patterns. By Thursday, an additional strategy unfolds in this scenario. If the ask has gone to $75, the market mood is now definitely optimistic. It would take some new information, or event surprises, to trigger a reversal of the trend direction. With 75 percent expected probability of success, the very same crowd-mind, which we tend to doubt as accurate on Monday, is much more reliable on Thursday. With only two days left to expiration, a binary option trade with a $75 ask represents a 25 percent return in two days. Not bad by any standard.

Last Chance: Very-Deep-in-the-Money Fridays

Initiating a trade on Friday is appropriate for loading up on a position. By Friday, probability streams have narrowed and reduced the opportunities to very deep-in-the-money plays, such as $85 to $90 asks. This means the market is very confident of a binary strike price settling at $100. While such plays return zero to 15 percent in a few hours, they also risk 85 to 90 percent. Trading this strategy requires a high level of technical confirmation.

A different view of binary option trading opportunities is worth considering—the once-a-month trade. Once every month, the nonfarm payroll data release moves the markets. A breakout strategy put on for the first week of every month (since the nonfarm payroll report comes out the first Friday of every month) may be all you need to satisfy the challenge and excitement of binary option trading.

Using Binaries with Forex Trading

An application worthy of much further analysis, but slightly beyond the scope of this book, is the use of binary options in combination with spot trading. Because binary options pay out a fixed amount if a strike price is penetrated, and settles in-the-money, they can be viewed as a form of rebate insurance. For example, if a trader had a long position in the EUR/USD spot market, he can also select a sell binary option strike price in which he would have placed a stop. If the EUR/USD sold off and he incurred losses in his spot account at the same time, the binary account would pay off. This can offset part or all of the loss.

One can view the binary option as a form of hedge as well when doing correlated trades. For example, if a trader was trading crude oil futures, she can at the same time put on a trade in the opposite direction on the USD/CAD. Remember, they are from a technical point of view inversely correlated. Being long on oil, and being wrong, would likely see the USD/CAD rise. Therefore, a trader being long on oil would also be long the USD/CAD binary to provide a form of a hedge. A USD/CHF trade may be used to hedge an S&P equity trade.

A Word on Intraday and Intra-Hour Strategies

So far, we have not directly discussed trading binaries, intraday or even intra-hour. Actually, there is no difference from a strategy point of view. These short-term duration trades enable the same strategies to be played but in a compressed time frame. An at-the-money bid/ask quote will still be essentially near $50 for an intraday binary. The difference, however, lies in the timing skills of the trader. Trading intraday requires very effective understanding of momentum, volatility, and technical analysis. In contrast, the weekly binary plays use fundamental analysis more effectively.

References

Cofnas, Abe. 2011. "Binary Update: More Reasons to Expect a Thursday Payoff," *Agora Financial* (January 26). http://strategiccurrencytrader.agorafinancial.com/2011/01/26/binary-update-more-reasons-to-expect-a-thursday-payoff/.

Bureau of Labor Statistics. 2011. "The Employment Situation—May 2011." News release from the Bureau of Labor Statistics (June 3). www.bls.gov/.

D'Amuri, Francesco, and Juri Marcucci. 2010. "Forecasting the U.S. Unemployment Rate with a Google Job Search Index." 2nd International Conference in Memory of Carlo Giannini Time Series Econometrics and Macroeconomic Forecasting in a Policy Environment, Rome (January 19). http://static.googleusercontent.com/external_content/untrusted_dlcp/research.google.com/en/us/archive/papers/initialclaimsUS.pdf

Federal Reserve Bank of Philadelphia. 2011. "Second Quarter 2011 Survey of Professional Forecasters." www.philadelphiafed.org/research-and-data/real-time-center/survey-of-professional-forecasters/2011/survq211.cfm.

Federal Reserve Bank of Philadelphia. 2015. "Fourth Quarter 2015 Survey of Professional Forecasters." https://www.philadelphiafed.org/research-and-data/real-time-center/survey-of-professional-forecasters/2015/survq415.

Kowalski, Alex, and Shobhana Chandra. 2011. "Jobless Claims in U.S. Unexpectedly Jump on One-Time Events," Bloomberg.com (May 5). www.bloomberg.com/news/2011-05-05/jobless-claims-in-u-s-unexpectedly-jump-due-to-special-factors.html.

Willis, Bob. 2011. "Initial Jobless Claims in U.S. Increase to Three-Month High." Bloomberg.com (April 28). www.bloomberg.com/news/2011-04-28/jobless-claims-in-u-s-unexpectedly-rise-to-three-month-high.html.

CHAPTER 9

Risk Management in Theory and Practice

We all know that there is no free lunch. The high returns offered by binary option trades are accompanied by risks. The goal of a good risk management program for binary option trading is not to eliminate risks. That is impossible. Each trader has to learn to balance the risks and the rewards. The task requires a handle on one's own personal risk curve as well as tactics that detect risk exposures in the price action. Let's first review some important aspects of personal risk psychology and management.

Consider the following scenario: It is Wednesday and you have put on a binary trade that can be closed at $70. What would you rather have: A sure 100-percent capture of the profit, or wait until Friday's expiration and try for a $100 payout, representing a return of 150 percent but possibly risk it all? What would you do? This is not that simple a question and what your answer would actually be is likely to change as you are navigating through your monthly performance. Actually, you have to ask yourself another question: What do you really care about in the trade? Are you only interested in the final value of the trade, or the trade itself becomes an experience that is worthy of the risk? Social scientists refer to the trader who cares only about the final value as operating under *expected utility theory (EUT)*. But research shows that people trade for more than just a final value. Many traders trade for entertainment value. Recent research published in an article titled "Why Do People Trade?" concluded: "Like lottery players who buy tickets with negative expected values, entertainment-driven investors trade even though trading diminishes the expected monetary payoff of their portfolio" (Dorn 2008). In other words: trading is fun. This particularly applies to binary option trading.

Deal or No Deal?

Let's play the game *Deal or No Deal*. To repeat the question: What would you rather have: A sure 100-percent capture of the profit, or wait until Friday's expiration and try for a $100 payout, representing a return of 150 percent but possibly risk it all? How you answer this question reveals a great deal about your risk attitude, preference, or your level of loss aversion, as well as how you should customize a risk management approach to your trading.

The first step in the binary options risk management plan is to identify your risk personality. Are you an all-or-nothing trader, putting on the trades and letting them go the distance with either a $100 or $0 payout? Or are you a leg-out trader, willing to get out at a sure 100 percent return and leave some lots on for the remaining duration? In the heat of the moment, in trading, very often what you planned goes out the window and what you do is a departure. It's important to realize that the reversal of risk preferences that occur in the middle of a trade is not necessarily a failure of planning; rather, it is the reality that trading decisions are not totally rational. Nor should they be. Traders operate instead with what social scientists have termed *bounded rationality*. Risk management becomes a process of satisfying behavior.

Trading binary options always involves emotional influences. They are not wrong. But few traders examine their inventory of emotions that affect their trading. The basic set of emotions that all of us have are also likely to be encountered during trading. These emotions include happiness, fear, disgust, and anger. While trading, ask yourself which of these emotions are affecting your entry and exit decisions. How many times will a trader get out of a position and leave profits on the table because of anger over a previous losing streak? Or, how many times will a trader be reticent about putting on a trade, because it is following a losing streak? Is a deep-out-of-the-money trade justified by a technical analysis process, or is it an outcome of a trader's instincts? When is optimism on a binary option trade excessive? We have to realize that risk control becomes more than the mathematics of profitability; it is also a process of managing emotions.

The Confidence Index

In an article in the *Journal of Behavioral Finance*, the authors discuss confidence: "Confidence in one's abilities is always helpful in one's achievements in life. But overconfidence in finance and investment may result in suboptimal decision making and inferior investment performance." Another leading work on behavioral finance by Max Bazerman (2008, 141) states: "Once people make an investment, they tend to be overly optimistic about its future profitability and later maintain optimistic recollection of the investment's past performance."

Therefore, you can see there is a tenuous balance between confidence and overconfidence. How can this balance be secured? There are many approaches for handling emotions in trading. In fact, an entire new field called neuroscience and finance has emerged to investigate how the human brain reacts to risk and reward. But at this point, the trader needs some practical guidance.

A good way to track your emotional decisions on your binary option trades is to rank each trade when you put it on. This simple task goes a long way to enabling you to evaluate the role of emotions in your trading results. Are you extremely confident? Give it a score of 5. Are you very confident, but not to the extreme? Give it a score of 4. Are you tentative but consider it worth trying? Give it a 3. However, if the ranking is less than 3 you should consider not trading it, because a rank of 2 and below is really being a contrarian to your own best judgment.

Ultimately, after a series of trades, you will be able to get a distribution of your initial confidence ranking against the outcome. If your emotional intelligence is strong, your most confident trades would show significantly more wins than losses. If you are a very intuitive trader, then your trades ranked 3 will show more than 50 percent wins.

Lot Size Management

A crucial trading decision rule is determining lot size or the size of the binary bet. One of the most common and dangerous mistakes made by binary option traders is putting on a big position because of overconfidence. Many traders also endanger their prospects of profitability because they put on trades in the absence of confirmations that the fundamental and technical conditions justify greater weight to the trade. There are several solutions to the problem of determining lot size.

First, let's consider the *rule of three*. The rule applies here to the number of lots that should be put on. This rule can be used for trading in many markets. Basically, the trader looks at position size in multiples of three. This means that there are several tactics for position size using this rule:

All In: This tactic is when the trader places three lots at one time on a binary option contract.

Partially In: This tactic is when the trader places a sequence of lots, one at a time.

Another risk-control approach, which is particularly important to traders of the offshore hi-low binaries, is not to risk more than 2 percent of equity on any binary option trade. Using this rule will clearly convey to traders that larger accounts are in fact safer. The reason larger accounts are safer is that a trader with a small account tends to put on more lots to generate a cash goal. She forgets the percentage risk she is taking on each trade. Getting out under the rule of three provides the following choices:

All Out: Closing all the positions.
Legging Out: Closing one or two positions during the week.

A critical question is: When do you place more lots on? As indicated earlier, it's not that easy a question to answer. Certainly one answer is to place more lots on when the trader has a high level of confidence with the position working out. But that confidence ultimately has to be based on a record of results. When starting out, there is no basis to be confident about your own level of confidence! Be patient because it takes more time. Another approach is based on the fear factor. Does the trader have a high risk tolerance and no fear of entirely losing the position? For example, a deep-in-the-money $85 option on Wednesday or Thursday may seem like a sure bet, but the risk is losing it all. Are you prepared to do so? Many beginning traders are trading with capital they really don't want to risk. A scenario that justifies higher risk is a situation in which the trader has built up some profits and at the end of the week or month is really risking the profits generated and not the principal.

The time of the week provides a rubric for risk control, especially for traders of binary ladders. An $80 binary option price on Monday is far riskier than an $80 binary option trade on Thursday. There is more time on Monday for things to go wrong. Conversely, a $25 binary option trade on Monday has less risk than a $25 binary option play on a Thursday. There is more time for things to go right! The high return pays off if new information surprises the market. Ultimately, it is a balance between fear and greed.

Offsetting Trades: Failing Forward

What about risk control when the markets are going the other way and the open positions are not working out? The scenario might be familiar to many: a position you believed would work out great is just out of energy and will not settle in-the-money. The result is a $0 payout and total loss of the position. The way to reduce the impact of this loss is to view the loss as a contra-directional signal. In other words, leave the position alone, and go the other way by putting on a position that goes with the market expectations either in the same underlying market or in a correlated one. This amounts to switching horses in the middle of the rate. The problem with this approach is more emotion than meets the eye. Traders tend to marry their positions and get attached to the ego factor in being right. Switching, to these traders, means admitting they are wrong. Yet, it's important to realize that the market doesn't care if the trader is right or wrong!

Leverage and Margin

Risk control is helped because of the fact that in binary option trading there is no margin. The amount traded cannot exceed the amount of cash in the account. A $10,000 account cannot have more than $10,000 purchased. If a trader is selling a $15 binary option with a bet that the strike price will not go above a certain level, the account will require that $85 be set aside to hold that position. Therefore, the most that can be risked, $85, is the amount of the margin calculated. It doesn't matter if there is a resting order. The tactical implications are relevant when the trader is putting on a large position, such as 50 lots. As soon as it is put on, the Nadex exchange or IG will consider the total margin to be calculated as if the entire position is filled. A working position, therefore, has the same margin requirements as a filled position.

References

Bazerman, Max, and Don Moore. 2008. *Judgment in Managerial Decision Making, Seventh Edition*. Hoboken, NJ: John Wiley & Sons.

Cheng, Philip Y. K. 2010. "Improving Financial Decision Making With Unconscious Thought: A Transcendent Model." *Journal of Behavioral Finance* 11 (2): 92–102.

Dorn, Anne, Daniel Dorn, and Paul Sengmueller. 2008. "Why Do People Trade?" *Journal of Applied Finance* (Fall/Winter): 49. www.washburn.edu/faculty/rweigand/page2/HWFiles/Why-Do-People-Trade.pdf.

CHAPTER 10

Metrics for Improving Binary Trading Performance

Evolving and improving your trading performance for binary options requires an ongoing commitment to evaluate one's own performance. Up to this point, this book has navigated through many strategies and tactics for trading binaries. The challenge is whether you have improved your skills. This chapter reviews key performance metrics that can guide you as you evolve your trading.

Key Performance Metrics

There are many variables involved in such evaluations. The following are some useful categories to keep in mind.

Win/Loss Ratio

As discussed earlier, the ability to become profitable is really a two-part equation. All levels of profitability ultimately relate to a win/loss ratio and an average profit/average loss ratio. The result is a personalized profitability curve that describes whether the trader is profitable and whether the trader is stable in maintaining profitability. Ask yourself after conducting a series of trades (10 or more): What does my profitability curve look like?

Adjusted Win/Loss Ratio

Ask yourself, what would happen to your performance if you removed from the calculation the best-winning and the worst-losing trade? This is called the adjusted win/loss ratio and adjusted average gain/average loss. It suggests a more realistic performance result than the original win/loss and average gain/average loss ratios. Don't be fooled by one great trade or one great loss. It's the adjusted win/loss ratio that is more indicative of your actual core skill level.

Near-Miss Ratio

In binaries, if you win by just the smallest margin, you are a winner and the same goes for losing by the smallest margin. This is why it is a good idea to measure how big your wins and losses are. If you win by large margins, then your confidence in the strategy you used can be reliable. If you lose by large margins, you can consider it a clue to improve your strategy. Therefore, count the near misses as a percentage of the win/loss ratio. The goal is to have as few as possible near misses and bigger size wins.

Distance from Breakeven

When all is said and done, it's about profitability. The goal, however, of getting profitable first requires getting beyond the breakeven point. A breakeven score is a very significant milestone. It means the trader is very close to profitability. Perhaps, it may be only a few changes, and profitability becomes more common. What is the key to breaking the breakeven barrier? It is consistency. The trader who is consistently wrong can at least identify one or two reasons for the performance problems. A trader who is flipping from profits to losses has a more difficult ability to diagnose the causes of their losses. Understanding the stability of your trading record is a key piece of information. What is the risk of ruin? What is the risk of losing your profits? Is it coming from one or two bad trades, or is it related to a strategy?

A first approach in evaluating one's performance and your risk exposure to losses is to determine how many trades it takes to break even (Figure 10.1). Another way to look at this is to understand that the path to profits must first cross the breakeven barrier. The following table shows costs per trade, maximum profit per trade, and maximum loss per trade (Table 10.1). For

FIGURE 10.1 Trades to Break Even

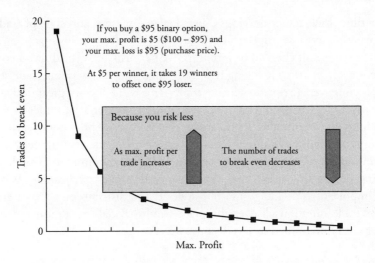

Max. Profit

each combination of these three, there is a number of winning trades it takes to reach a breakeven point. In other words, any number less means that the trade is not profitable. For example, if a trader buys a $95 binary option, it will take 19 winners to offset one $95 loser!

TABLE 10.1 Breakeven Points in Trading

Cost of Trade	Maximum Profit	Maximum Loss	Winning Trades to Break Even
90	10	90	9.00
85	15	85	5.67
80	20	80	4.00
75	25	75	3.00
70	30	70	2.33
65	35	65	1.86
60	40	60	1.50
55	45	55	1.22
50	50	50	1.00
45	55	45	0.82
40	60	40	0.67
35	65	35	0.54

Win/Loss Duration

Over time, each trader develops a personalized pattern and style of trading. There are patterns within the winning trades, as well as the losing trades, that provide important clues on how to improve performance. The duration of the trade is a key metric. How long is your average time in a winning trade? How long is your average time in a losing trade? This will tell you a great deal about your psychological profile as a trader. If you are a set-and-let trader, you will have long duration trades. If you are on the other side of the trader-style continuum, you will have short trades, revealing a frenetic trading personality. It's important to note that there is no good or bad connotation with your trading personality; it is a clue as to how to improve your trading. What is also important is a change in your style. If the distribution of your trades shows trade duration all over the place (multi-modal), it indicates you are either a very diversified or a very confused trader!

Trading Sequence Patterns

Every trader has winning and losing streaks. It's part of the game. However, each trader has his or her own maximum winning and losing streaks in his or her trading history. This tells you a great deal. If you are near your previous maximum winning streak, it's a good idea to be careful, because you're at a high probability of ending that streak. Winning streaks are more than just being right about the market—they are also about your total mind-set and emotional intelligence in trading. Near the end of a winning streak, traders get overconfident, overzealous, and start making strategic and technical mistakes. Likewise, into a losing streak, each loss wears on the trader and affects judgments as to the next trade.

Another aspect of trading-sequence patterns that is important to note and review is the sequence of win, lose, win, lose. This sequence shows difficulty in performance, and may become a precursor to the beginning of a losing streak.

Strategy Scorecard

Binary option trading performance is not only a statistical outcome, it is a result of using strategies. This means that any performance review can be evaluated from a strategy point of view. The best way to do this is to distribute your trading results by the five main strategies used: at-the-money (ATM), out-of-the-money (OTM), deep-out-of-the-money (DOOM), in-the-money (ITM), and deep-in-the-money (DITM). Look at your trading history and determine which are your best and worst trades from a strategy point of view.

YOUR PERFORMANCE SCORECARD

To help you effectively evaluate your binary option trading performance, you can use a binary option trader scorecard as a key tool. It reviews your trading history and produces a report card on key parameters of your performance. Go to www .binarydimensions.com for more details.

Performance Challenges

A static backward-looking review of your binary option trading performance is useful but it's really only a first step to moving ahead. The next part of the process of evaluating your performance is by testing your results on a forward-looking, real-time basis. This means planning and putting on trades with a strategy in mind. Think of it as a training schedule for a binary option trading marathon. It is a fast track to improved performance because binary option trading is not a game of chance. The probability of improving performance is related to your skills and not the market.

Each performance challenge tests a core binary option trading skill. Ultimately, the trader will discover his or her strengths and choose strategies that play to that skill.

There is no single strategy that applies to everyone. Each trader applies his or her own personality to the trading and only after many trades can a real trading plan emerge. Until that happens, the trader needs to look at his or her own trading as a self-improvement path to obtain trading fitness.

When completed, the results of these exercises will provide you the equivalent of a blood test of your binary option trading skills. The size of the account doesn't matter. A trader can do one challenge over one week or take more time. It is important to have a big enough account to place trades at a frequency that gives the trader exposure to changing market conditions. One trade a week won't take the sample frequency to a level sufficient to evaluate with any forecast accuracy. So it will take a balance of size and frequency. Consider the following list of performance challenges for laddered binary trading.

1. **Ten ATM Trades:** The challenge here is to see how good you are in timing entry. ATM trades are essentially momentum-based trades.
2. **Ten ITM Trades:** The challenge here is to join the crowd after confirming a strong trend direction. The ITM trades cost more than $75. This makes it more important to be right more often. The risk is that one or two poor trades can wipe out your gains.
3. **Ten OTM Trades:** If you are a contrarian, OTM trades are for you. They are low cost, about $15 to $30, but they pay out very large returns. The key skill here is to understand price patterns signaling a breakout or reversal. The trader is essentially betting against the crowd.
4. **Ten DOOM Trades:** Deep-out-of-the-money strategies are appropriately named DOOM. It's for high rollers who buy $10 to $20 ask prices. The key is, what is your mathematics of performance? Are you on the right side of your profitability curve? The mission here is to find out.
5. **Ten DITM Trades:** Deep-in-the-money trades are high-probability wins, but there is a high cost to being wrong. The real challenge is to see how good you really are at spotting a stable trend continuation.
6. **Ten Gut Trades:** Gut trades are trades based on the blink effect. This is to quickly scan the markets and make an instinctive judgment about direction. This exercise is designed to help avoid paralysis-by-analysis syndrome. Don't overanalyze. This exercise will often provide a benchmark for your emotional intelligence.
7. **Ten Headline Trades:** Look at the headlines in the *Financial Times*, Google, and Bloomberg and use your sentiment-assessment skills to find the right trading direction.
8. **Ten Contrarian Trades:** In this performance challenge, the task is to deliberately go against the crowd. The crucial question is: When is the crowd wrong?
9. **Ten Bounce Trades:** Try to find sideways channels, and put on trades anticipating a failure to break through both resistance and support.
10. **Ten Breakout Trades:** Try to find a sideways channel and put on a pair of binary trades that anticipate a breakdown of support or a breakout of resistance.
11. **Ten Data Release Trades:** Specifically locate the economic calendar for an important data release, such as the non-farm payroll or a key central bank report. Put on a binary play on the day of the release with a 50 percent profit-taking target.
12. **Thirty Mixed-Strategy Trades:** After you have done the first 11 strategy tests, look at the results and pick out the three best strategies and put on

30 trades (yes, three times the usual number), testing with 10 trades for each of the three best strategies.

13. **Ten Directional Trades:** On the U.S. market opening, watch the S&P 500 and based on its direction, trade the same direction on the USD/ JPY. On the Shanghai Opening, watch the Shanghai Index and on the direction of the opening, trade the same direction on the AUD/USD. Watch the direction of U.S. crude (WTI) and trade the USD/CAD in the opposite direction.

These performance challenges are designed to provide milestones for evolving as a binary option trader. The results of each performance challenge set provide important data to assess strengths and weaknesses. Go to www.binarydimensions.com for more performance challenges and to submit your results.

Performance Challenges for Trading High-Low Binaries

For binary option traders trading platforms that offer only the high-low type of trades, the following performance challenges will help test your skills.

1. For one-minute binary expirations, turn on one-minute three-line break charts and trade when you see a reversal of colors.
2. For five-minute binary expirations, wait for a parabolic curve to be formed and trade the opposite direction once it reaches a peak and then starts reversing. Trade a 15-minutes expiration.
3. For a 30-minute binary expiration, locate an underlying market that has a sideways range of about 30 pips and place a double Bollinger Band on it. Wait for the price to reach the outer band and then reverse. Then put a 30-minute expiration on the direction of the reversal.

Analytical Challenges

While putting on trades is ultimately the best form of testing your skills, it's important to also challenge your analytical abilities. The following analytical challenges are evergreen. They do not go out of date and can be done anytime.

- What is the sentiment of the market regarding the U.S. dollar (DXY)? Is it risk averse or risk appetite, and why?

- Scan the binary option underlying markets for markets that just reached new weekly highs. What is the reason for the new highs?
- Among the floating currencies, what are the widest interest-rate differentials?
- What is your adjusted win/loss ratio (remove the highest gain and the highest loss, and then recompute the result)?
- Scan the four-hour charts of the underlying markets and select one that has a compressed triangle forming. Put on a breakout trade around that triangle.
- On Thursday, 10 A.M. EST, find three different underlying binary trade option strike prices that are being offered at $75 and put one lot on each to test the strategy of going with the crowd.
- Find the underlying market that hit new weekly lows. What is the reason for the new lows?
- Compare the S&P 500, Shanghai Composite Index, and on their past three-month performance. Which pair is the most divergent?
- On the next Wednesday, choose three underlying markets and find the ATM bid/ask. Choose the one that is most likely, in your opinion, to go from ATM to ITM and place a trade with a 50 percent profit limit.
- Find two underlying markets that have had a very narrow sideways channel in the past month. Place a breakout trade on each market.
- Conduct a review of headlines on the U.S. dollar and develop your own risk appetite/risk aversion sentiment ratio.
- Locate and review the nonfarm payroll jobless claims data and determine if there is a trend up or down in the data.
- Determine on the economic calendar when the next Tankan report is coming out.
- Do a scan of the currency pairs and evaluate their three-line break patterns. Which pair has just experienced a three-line break reversal using the one-week chart?
- Which of the underlying markets are experiencing a sideways one-week channel?
- Find the appropriate ETF for the underlying market and locate the at-the-money put/call ratio. Is it skewing to the bearish or the bullish side?
- Look at the gold/oil ratio. Is it at an extreme?
- Check the Shanghai Index and overlay it against the AUD/USD. Try to predict next week's direction.
- Go to the central bank of Switzerland (www.snb.ch) and read their monetary policy. Find out when was the last time they raised interest rates.

- Find the binary option strike prices that are near the 61.8 percent weekly or daily Fibonacci resistance lines.

Look Online

For more information on binary option trading analytical challenges, go to:

www.binarydimensions.com.

Useful strategies for charting can be found at:

www.livecharts.co.uk
www.prorealtime.com

Know Your Trading Personality

Part of the evolution of success in getting better at binary option trading is to understand your own trader personality. The fact is it is impossible to separate emotions from the trade. This is a fact of life and the challenge is to recognize one's own personality. This will help limit your risks by associating the trading strategy that calibrates to your personality. There are several personality types and the field of psychological finance is devoting a lot of work to modeling emotions and how they become translated into the traits of a trader. In fact, an entire new field called *computational psychology and artificial chemistry* is focused on mapping how emotions result in behavior. A good place to start to detect your trading personality is to consider which of the following archetypes best calibrates with you.

> **The Gladiator/Samurai**—This person loves to trade even more than winning or losing. Being in the action is the objective. We call them the gladiator-type because gladiators had no fear of death and focused on the battle itself. A gladiator-type of binary option trader has the advantage of being committed to the trade without being frenetic about the result. The disadvantage of this personality is that it can lead to overtrading and unnecessary losses. Few gladiators survive for long!
>
> **The Warrior**—This personality type loves trading but really wants to win. He avoids trades that are not highly probable and has no allegiance to any one market. This type of personality is comfortable with a mixed binary option strategy, each one being a different weapon of choice.

The Gunslinger/Surfer—He or she acts upon an emotional or gut feeling to enter or exit a trade. This type of personality often likes to surf and jump from one trading opportunity to another. At-the-money, momentum-type strategies attract this personality.

The Sniper—Analyzes the market and takes the trade only when the market moves on the conditions they have specified. This trading style is similar to swing trading or waiting for a key support or resistance level to be tested. Many people do not have the patience, or the wisdom, to be a sniper-trader. This type favors breakout trades that provide out-of-the-money pricing.

The Lamb—This type of trader reacts to market moves by running with the crowd. When a lot of such traders come into the market, they add energy to the momentum of the prices, creating a contagion. Deep-in-the-money binary option trades are favored by this personality.

The Black Sheep—The trading behavior of this personality is contrarian. This type of trader doesn't join the crowd and seeks an opposite opportunity. It takes courage to be a black sheep. But when the black sheep is right, profits are very large.

The Gambler—This person's attitude toward trading is similar to that of a gambler. The motivation is not to seek a profitable return. The trader is in it as a search for excitement at the moment. He or she is not distressed by losses.

The Eagle—This type of trader scans multiple markets and multiple time frames to determine best possible trading opportunity. The Eagle trader is a predator that is in impulsive.

The Donkey—The donkey trader experiences consecutive losses and doesn't change the strategy. He or she is stubborn like a mule.

Self-examination of one's own trading personality will provide many insights that can improve your results. Very often, the critical weakness facing the binary option trader is not a lack of technical, or fundamental analysis, but a lack of being aware of the psycho-dynamics relating to the trade.

Targeting Total Returns

Trading performance can be viewed on a trade-by-trade basis, but it can also be viewed from total-return perspective. This later approach is more a top-down approach and, in fact, makes a huge difference on how each trade is viewed. The bottom-up approach looks at each trade as its own self-contained opportunity. In contrast, the top-down approach views each trade as a component toward a total return per week or per month. Each trade is, metaphorically, a component in a trading factory. The question arises: What's the production of the factory for each week or month—in terms of total return.

There are different ways to approach binary option trading from a total return perspective, and all are legitimate because they reflect the belief that traders have varying goals. Some traders seek the opportunity to put on a position for a very high return. These traders are high rollers, with large risk appetites. This kind of trader searches for binary contracts that offer the opportunity to pay out a $100 on a risk of $20 (therefore delivering 5:1 returns in less than a week). In contrast, the other group of traders is looking for high-probability returns. For them, binary option contracts that cost $75 and higher are often attractive. They offer less reward, but have a higher probability of success.

Whether one trades for high returns or high probability, there are two distinctive total return perspectives. You can view binary options on a trade-by-trade basis and enjoy the experience. An analogy would be doing a round of golf, but not keeping score. Another approach is a total return portfolio approach. This means using binary options as a mechanism for achieving a total-return goal.

The total-return approach, in effect, reverses the process of shaping the binary option trade. Instead of starting with a scan of the market and identifying price patterns and opportunities, the trader starts by setting total return portfolio goals. This approach is a manufacturing model. It views traders as managers of a manufacturing process that produces profits per year, month, and week. Here are three questions that help you shape a binary option portfolio return plan. Ultimately, all total-return strategies can become translated into how you answer these questions.

1. What is your total return goal for a year?
2. What is your total return goal for a month?
3. What is your total return goal for a week?

For example, a 50-percent total return for one year of trading is a result that is not only admirable, but that places one among the better traders in the world. This results in a 4.1 percent return per month, or just over 1 percent a week. Having shaped a performance goal for the week, the next step is to develop a set of binary option trading strategies that contribute to that objective. Here is an example, in Table 10.2, of one week's trades that resulted in a 1 percent return for the week.

TABLE 10.2 Simulated Total Return Goal of 1 Percent per Week, Example for Week of April 25 to 29

Binary Option Contracts Traded (Expiration)			Cost	Settlement	P/L
U.S. 500 (JUN). 1311.5 (4:15 P.M.)	Buy	1	83	100	17
EUR/USD. 1.4275 (3 P.M.)	Buy	2	85.5	100	14.5
USD/CHF. 0.8925 (3 P.M.)	Buy	2	26.5	100	253
USD/CHF. 0.8875 (3 P.M.)	Sell	1	21.5	100	21.5
GBP/JPY. 1.6275 (3 P.M.)	Buy	1	86	100	14
GBP/USD. 1.6275 (3 P.M.)	Buy	1	87.5	100	12.5
USD/CAD. 0.9425 (3 P.M.)	Buy	1	84	100	16
CRUDE OIL (JUN). 106.75 (2.30 P.M.)	Buy	5	89.5	100	52.5
CRUDE OIL (JUN). 116.75 (2.30 P.M.)	Sell	5	10.5	0	52.5
GOLD (JUN). 1486.5 (1:30 P.M.)	Buy	1	85.5	100	14.5
U.S. 500 (JUN). 1353.5 (4:15 P.M.)	Buy	1	25	51.5	26.5

The 1 percent-per-week results would be competitive with any world-class manager, but by using the binary option trading tools, they are within the reach of ordinary persons. The example represents a sample set of trades, but it is still instructive. What can we learn from it? First, that binary option trading strategies are not a single pure strategy. The trades represent a combination of deep-in-the-money trades, at-the-money, and breakout trades. Of course, there are many combinations possible. Only after conducting a large number of trades per strategy can the best personal mixed strategy for any trader be developed.

Let's look at a possible combination set of trades or recipe that would result in a 1 percent return for the week (Figure 10.2). In reality, there are many ways to accomplish this, but it is suggestive of what it takes. The inputs are trades, and the trades result in a total cost. The output, if profitable, should be enough winners with big enough size wins to result in a net profit. In a real sense this is a recipe for a 1 percent weekly total return for a $10,000 account.

The results of the preceding hypothetical two-strategy combination provide insights into the challenges for the trader. Returns of 1 percent per week are the kind of return potential that no one should ignore. Let's consider the mathematics of profitability using this combination. The deep-in-the-money strategy needs to be 80 percent effective, and the deep-out-of-the-money strategy needs to be 60 percent effective. The results are sensitive to the cost of entry, of course. But you get the idea.

FIGURE 10.2 Simulated 1 Percent 1 Total Return in Week

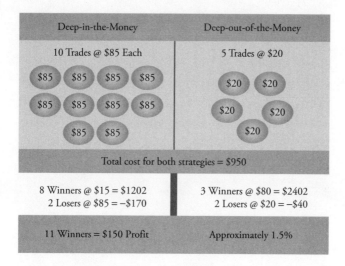

While the example refers to a 1 percent return, the binary option market can in fact result in much larger returns. For example, during the week of June 25 to 29, global markets moved greatly. Almost any binary option strategy worked very well for that week. The lesson is that when markets move in a synchronous direction and the trader is on the right side of the direction, enormous returns are possible. These results also point to the power of a mixed strategy. It provides a recipe for a variety of total return targets. It places trading strategy as a tool for accomplishing a goal, and not just a particular trade. But before a trader can effectively build and hone a binary option trading strategy, she must know how to evaluate her own trading performance.

CHAPTER 11

Performance Tools and Training for Improving Binary Option Trading

This chapter provides guidance on how to move beyond a beginner's level in binary trading. As the binary trading industry has grown, so has the number of robot programs and advisory services. We review key features of algorithmic trading and other performance aids such as alerts and trading competitions.

Algorithmic Trading: Is It for You?

Algorithmic trading defines sets of rules that determine the entry and exit points for positions. Automation of these rules helps traders achieve consistent returns while limiting both risk and emotion. Developing a system to trade binary options is not easy, but it is certainly a tool of the future. A binary trading and alert algorithm is now being developed using these principles and will soon be part of the binary options toolbox.

Advantages and Disadvantages of Automated Trading

Algorithmic trading, or automated trading, has several benefits, but it also has downsides. In fact, at this juncture in the evolution of technical analysis and trading, there is an ongoing debate. On one side are the "click traders," who make trades using their human instincts and intelligence. On the other side are the "bot traders," that are systems that trade at a high frequency. It is now estimated that 70 percent of trades are system-based. We don't know who will win the battle, but at this point, the human trader is behind in volume. However, it is arguable if systems can, in fact, replace the trader. In any case, binary options will become an area in which systems and alerts will be developed and offered. It is relevant to explore this area a bit further. Let's compare the main advantages and disadvantages of binary option trading on an algorithmic-based system.

The main advantages are:

- An automated approach takes the emotion and manual effort out of trading. This allows you to focus on improving your approach, rule sets, and money-management rules.
- A profitable system requires no work until it breaks, or market conditions demand a change. All systems go through cycles of good and bad. This is expected, but a time will come when the approach fails to recover and needs to be reviewed and redesigned.

And the main disadvantages are:

- If the system is not properly developed and tested, losses can happen very quickly and wipe out your confidence and trading account. This is particularly true for binary options, as binary options are a relatively recent development.
- Many times it is impossible to take into account every intricate rule you see while watching the screen.

We can see that it's useful to carefully review whether the algorithm-based system one has in mind reflects more of the advantages or disadvantages. Let's review the elements in developing such a system.

Developing a Trading System

There are several important steps involved in developing a binary option trading system: get the highest quality data, develop rules, test those rules, test in real time, and trade in a real account. This section discusses each step in closer detail.

Get the Data

All systems are developed and optimized against historical data. In every case, and with every system, data is king. A bad approach with questionable data could test fantastic but implode in real-time trading because you set parameters based on bad trade data. A great approach tested on bad data could test fantastic and implode in real trading for the same reason. So, you have to get the highest quality data possible.

Develop the Rules

There are four basic rules for every trading system:

1. **Buy Entry:** Where you want to open a new long position.
2. **Sell Entry:** Where you want to open a new short position.
3. **Stop Loss:** Where you want to cut your losses and exit the position.
4. **Profit Target:** Where you want to book your profits.

Every system uses some combination of these basic rules. For binaries, a sample rule for the EUR/USD may be: when the 21-day moving average of the underlying EUR/USD spot crosses the 50-day moving average of the EUR/USD spot—buy an at-the-money call option. (Note: This is only an example and not a suggested rule.)

The key to remember is that almost any indicator and trading rule that you currently use can be used within a trading system. The most important aspect is clarifying exactly what trading rule you want. It has to be quantifiable.

Test the Rules

Testing is a key step in the development of any approach. After you develop your rules, you need to start testing. Testing is not simply operating the algorithm and generating the results. Rather, it requires patience and structure.

Caution: Testing can create a false sense of security. You can minimize this by what is called, *in-sample testing* and *out-of-sample testing*.

In simple terms, you split your data into two parts. The first part, the in-sample data set, is designated for your base testing. You need to experiment with different combinations and take careful notes on the outcome of each test. From this work, you should arrive at rules, stop loss, and profit targets that produce the most consistent results.

Then take this rule set and test it against your out-of-sample data set. Hopefully, if you have been careful in your rules, note taking, and combination selection, you should achieve similar results for your in-sample and out-of-sample testing.

Test in Real Time

After you have developed and tested your system against historical data, it's time to put it to the real test and run it against real-time data. This is a critical step for a lot of reasons. First, it gives you peace of mind before you risk capital and it enhances the probability for account preservation. Second, back-testing doesn't provide a test of the real-world transaction environment in which there may be variations in the spread and in the ability to fill trades. It's a good idea to first set up a real-time test with a demo account, as long as the demo account is receiving real-time live quotes. As you watch the system trade, ensure the system acts and trades as expected and verify that it's trading as it did in all your previous testing. It's also important to determine the resources the algorithm or system will need to perform well.

Moving to a Live Account

The move to a live account is the biggest leap. However, at this point, you have developed and tested a set of rules and verified them against a live market. You are as prepared as you can be to put your approach to the test.

There are two basic methods for bringing the fruits of your labor live:

1. **Semi-Automated:** Semi-automated systems alert you when new trades are triggered. While the alerts are automated, the trades are not automatically placed. While this method carries less risk, there are downsides: (1) it requires you to be available to execute the trade when triggered, and (2), it allows your emotion to question the validity of the trade.
2. **Fully Automated:** Automated systems place trades in your account automatically and require no intervention on your part. There are risks. However, if you have taken the time to test the automated system in a demo account, you should have some added confidence in the execution and results.

In all cases, it is important to remember that you are still ultimately in control. If the system starts to implode or strays outside your testing boundaries, turn it off and regroup. Tomorrow is another day.

Evolving Your Approach

This is a brief walk-through of the basic steps involved for creating an automated trading system. There are entire books and a variety of sources written on the topic. There are also numerous professionals who can help turn your vision into reality.

As you continue to evolve your approach and system, keep these keys in mind: back-test, redesign, back-test, and back-test some more. If your system does not perform on historical data, there is no reason it will perform well on real-time data.

Once it trades well on historical data, run it long enough to validate that it's trading correctly on real-time data. Testing against years of historical data, then testing it in real time for a week is not validation. If your back-test encompassed 1,000 trades, test in real time until you see 100 trades.

Keep it simple. Extremely complex trading approaches often work extremely well with past data, but are too brittle for real-time market conditions.

Most importantly, know the strategy behind your trading system. As strange as it sounds, many people develop approaches, add bits and pieces, and eventually lose sight of their underlying strategy.

Using Alerts

Another method for trying to enhance one's binary option performance is to use alerts. Alerts can be automatic signals that indicate a buy or sell opportunity. Binary alerts can also specify which expiration should be used with the buy or sell alert. For example, momentum trades should be associated with next or expirations of relatively short periods, such as five minutes and 30 minutes. The challenge for automatic alerts that have emerged in the global market is that they are usually based on simplistic methods that have not really been proven.

A better alternative is to select an alert service that is offered by a trading expert. My newsletter site, www.binarydimensions.com, offers weekly binary option alerts and analysis on a Monday morning for Friday expiration. A separate alert service is also offered, as is trading China A50 on the Nadex exchange. These are weekly, daily, and intraday expirations. The China A50 track and the Shanghai Index offer an opportunity to trade the China market at night, after 9 P.M. EST. These alerts provide a basis for learning how to trade laddered binaries as well as gaining insight into predicted directions for the coming week. The following 100 percent winning binary alert recently occurred, demonstrating that extraordinary returns per week are possible with binary options (Table 11.1).

TABLE 11.1   Weekly Binary Alerts with All Winners

Date Expired	Trade Buy/Sell	Contract	Bid/Ask	Lots	Expiration Value	Win/Loss	Profit/Loss
1/29/16	SELL	USD/JPY > 121.25	10.50	−1	121.107	WIN	10.50
1/29/16	BUY	USD/JPY > 116.25	83.00	+2	121.07	WIN	17.00
1/29/16	BUY	GOLD (Apr) > 1101.5	59.00	+1	1116.8	WIN	41.00
1/29/16	BUY	CRUDE OIL (May) > 28.75	81.75	+1	33.662	WIN	18.25
1/29/16	BUY	AUD/USD > 0.7025	40.50	+1	0.70685	WIN	59.50
1/29/16	SELL	USD/CAD > 1.4475	12	−1	1.40114	WIN	12.00
1/29/16	BUY	USD/CAD > 1.3975	82	+1	1.40114	WIN	18.00

Source: www.binarydimensions.com.

Algo Alerts Trading Competitions

An emerging method for improving one's binary option trading is social trading. In social trading, a trader watches other traders and tries to copy their trades. An effective learning experience using social trading is trading competitions. This allows a trader to test one's skills in a trading contest. Some brokerage firms offer contests, mostly however, as a marketing gimmick to attract an account. In contrast, the site's unique opportunity allows traders to trade real binary option markets of various durations in a virtual account for prizes. Traders play a variety of challenges (best trader of the day, most consecutive winners, and so forth). Prizes are offered along with education. The platform is free and advanced educational opportunities are offered as well. Competitions require a minimal entry fee, such as $10.

Afterword

My hope with this book is that binary options becomes understood as a powerful tool for trading for beginners and experienced persons. The coming years will see greater than ever integration of global markets with instant and often emotional responses augmented by the Internet. As a result, fundamental forces that often took months to evolve and surface have greater salience than ever. In this context, binary options provide the trader the ability to navigate these increasingly volatile waters every week.

Good luck trading!

Appendix A:
Test Your Knowledge

It is always a good idea to test your trading knowledge and skills. One of the reasons this book has been written is to give you a jump-start. Let's see how much you have learned. There are 50 questions.

1. A binary option contract provides a fixed payout of:

    A. $15
    B. $100
    C. $50
    D. $200

2. A binary option trade cannot be traded before its expiration date.

    A. True
    B. False

3. If a trader was short a binary contract at a bid of $25, what amount did the trader have to put up in his or her account?

    A. $0
    B. $25
    C. $75
    D. $100

4. During the week, a trader went long the binary contract. The bid was $15 and the ask was $20. What did he or she or she pay for the contract (excluding fees)?

    A. $10
    B. $100 – $10
    C. $100 – $15
    D. $20

5. If, in a binary contract, the bid was at $33 and the ask was at $35, this means:

   A. The probability of the contract being in-the-money is 33 percent.
   B. The probability of the contract being in-the-money is 35 percent.
   C. The probability of the contract being in-the-money is 77 percent.
   D. The probability of the contract being in-the-money is not known.

6. If a trader was short a binary contract and the price settled at the binary strike price, the payoff would be _____.

   A. $0
   B. $35
   C. $50
   D. $100

7. During the week a trader went long the binary contract. The bid was $10 and the ask was $15. What kind of strategy was being employed?

   A. At-the-money
   B. In-the-money
   C. Deep-in-the-money
   D. Deep-out-of-the-money

8. If, in a binary contract, the bid was at $23 and the ask was at $25, this means

   A. The probability of the contract winning by the end of the week is 23 percent.
   B. The probability of the contract being in-the-money is 25 percent.
   C. The probability of winning by middle of the week is 77 percent.
   D. The probability of the contract being in-the-money is 75 percent.

9. A nonfarm payroll data release is scheduled for which day?

   A. First Friday of the month
   B. Second Friday of the month
   C. Third Friday of the month
   D. Last Friday of the month

10. The economic calendar is listing a key speech by Trichet. Which currency pair is most likely to be affected?

   A. British Pound/Dollar
   B. Dollar/Canadian
   C. European Central Bank
   D. Aussie/Dollar

11. A trader has an account of $15,000 and places five binary option contracts, costing a total of $1,500. The percentage of leverage is approximately:

    A. 3:1
    B. 1:2.5
    C. 5:1
    D. 1:1

12. A trader completes 10 binary trades with one lot on each trade. The result is four winners. What needs to be the average loss of each trade to break even?

    A. $30
    B. $40
    C. $22
    D. $43

13. The trader sees the spot market for a currency pair at 1.4650 on Monday morning. He believes the trend is going down. The Nadex binary option strike that would be cheapest to sell is

    A. 1.4500
    B. 1.4550
    C. 1.4600
    D. 1.5750

14. The trader observes a sideways channel in an underlying market. He believes the price action will feature a breakout of the channel. Which of the current strategies could be used?

    A. Choose a binary contract with a strike price outside the support.
    B. Choose a binary contract with a strike price outside the resistance.
    C. Choose a binary contract with the strike price in the middle.

15. If a price is in a steady sideways action, which pattern best describes this?

    A. Equilateral triangle
    B. Channel pattern
    C. Parabolic curve
    D. Descending triangle

16. Which price action is not associated with the pattern?

    A. Channel Pattern—Breakout Trade
    B. Equilateral Triangle—Breakout Trade
    C. Parabolic Curve—Retracement

17. The trader sees that the jobless claims data release will occur later in the week on Thursday. He is bullish on the economy and therefore wants to choose which strike price?

    A. 155,000
    B. 175,000
    C. 123,000
    D. Can't answer

18. The trader is interested in a crude oil trade. He believes the problems in the Middle East will settle down. The spot price is $103.20. Which strike price should she look at?

    A. WTI crude oil 104.50
    B. Nymex crude oil 101.00
    C. Brent crude oil 104.50
    D. WTI crude oil 101.00

19. Two binary option traders are comparing their performance. Joe has 10 trades with seven winners and three losers. Bob has 10 trades with five winners and five losers. Who is the more profitable trader?

    A. Joe
    B. Bob
    C. Can't tell from the information

20. The news comes out and oil surges. Bob wants to play this market but is afraid of trading oil binaries. Which other contract can he trade that plays best off oil?

    A. S&P 500
    B. AUD/USD
    C. USD/CAD
    D. EUR/USD

21. The trader is bearish on the U.S. dollar and wants to put on a binary trade shorting the dollar. Which of the following orders reflects a bearish dollar direction?

    A. Short USD/CAD
    B. Long GBP/USD
    C. Short USD/JPY
    D. Long EUR/USD

22. The trader is bullish on copper and expects a big data release on copper supply. He doesn't, however, want to be directly in copper. Which of the following moves with copper movements?

    A. USD/CHF
    B. USD/CAD
    C. AUD/USD
    D. U.S. 500

23. A trader is short a binary contract; the bid is $33 and the ask is $38. They put on a short position of one contract. They want to get out with a profit of 50 percent. What trading price should the ask position be to achieve this result?

    A. $67
    B. $19
    C. $83.5
    D. $15

24. A trader draws weekly support and resistance levels to determine which binary strike price to choose. They want to go long the position and notices that the price of binary they are interested in is just above the 61.8 percent weekly Fib line. As a result, he chooses the binary contract that is below the 61.8 percent Fib line to improve the technical conditions to achieve their results. Do you agree with this decision?

25. Mark wants to trade the nonfarm payroll, but decides not to play the nonfarm payroll directly, so he instead selects the U.S. 500 contract. Which two of the following contracts is the best to trade on this news event?

    A. EUR/USD
    B. USD/CHF
    C. USD/CAD
    D. AUD/USD

26. If a trader wants to trade the Indian stock market, which of the underlying contracts should she choose?

    A. Liffe FTSE 100 Index Futures
    B. SGX Nifty Index Futures
    C. Kospi 200 Index Futures
    D. SGX Nikkei Futures

27. A trader went long a binary contract and the price settled right at the binary strike price. What was the settlement value?

    A. $0
    B. $100
    C. $50
    D. $25

28. A trader has a long binary position on and it is Friday morning. The position has reached $90 and the trader decides to leave it to expiration. Which of the following reasons makes the most sense for this decision?

    A. The underlying market went into a five-minute parabolic pattern.
    B. The underlying market broke above its 50 percent daily Fib line.
    C. The trader simply wants to take his profits and not risk a sell off.

29. Mark has a trading performance in which he has a 50 percent win record for the past 20 trades and an average profit of $50 per win. His losses average $80. How profitable is he?

    A. $500
    B. $300
    C. $250
    D. $0

30. A trader is looking for the two strike prices that are equal in probability if one was sold and the other was bought. He or she is interested in a trade that plays the price staying in the range, but wants to choose the strike prices based on equal probabilities. Which of the following should they choose?

    A. Long the $15 ask and long the $85 ask.
    B. Short the $15 ask and short the $85 ask.
    C. Short the $85.

31. The European Central Bank is anticipated to increase interest rates and announce it on Wednesday. Brian, a trader decides to trade it. He believes there will be no increase in the rate that will surprise the market. Which of the following describes a straddle position?

    A. Buy a binary strike price slightly at-the-money and sell a binary strike price at-the-money.
    B. Buy a binary strike price slightly out-of-the-money and sell a binary strike price slightly below-the-money.

32. A trader realizes that there is a lot of volatility in the market. Which of the following indicators could they use to help determine if volatility is increasing or decreasing?

    A. Fibonacci levels
    B. Bollinger Bands
    C. VIX Index
    D. MACD

33. Which of the following technical conditions confirm a bearish direction?

    A. Price has risen, gone beyond a 61.8 percent day Fib line, and turned back down.
    B. A descending triangle has been detected.
    C. The underlying market is in a parabolic rise.

34. Mary opens an account with $10,000 and puts an order to buy 25 USD/JPY binary options at the ask price of $15. Three of the orders were filled. How much margin does she have left?

    A. $9,975
    B. $0
    C. $9,250
    D. $10,000

35. Two binary strike prices are equally distant from the spot market. One is above the spot and the other is below the spot. Will they have the same bid/ask trade price?

    A. Never
    B. Always
    C. Maybe
    D. Not enough information to determine

36. Ted wants to trade the hourly binary on one of the markets. Bob likes to stay with the weekly. Bob tells Ted that the hourly is too risky and offers a reduced payout. Is Bob correct?

    A. Yes
    B. No

37. What is the main difference between binary option trading on the Nadex and with OTC firms?

    A. Nadex trading prices on bids and asks are the same no matter which brokerage firm a trader is using to put on the trade.

    B. The spread between the bid and ask at Nadex is likely to be narrower than OTC firms.

    C. Nadex does not offer one-touch options.

38. Who is the market maker for Nadex binary contracts?

    A. SEC

    B. CFTC

    C. NASDAQ

    D. IG Markets

39. Bob has put on a GBP/USD binary option trade for the week. Mary has noticed that there is a Monetary Policy Committee (MPC) minutes report to be released during the week. Bob says that that is just a report and not important. Do you agree with Bob?

    A. Yes

    B. No

40. A trader buys a binary option contract at strike price 1.45 and wants to put a stop position on the binary contract. Which of the following orders should he use as a stop order?

    A. Sell stop 1.40

    B. Sell to close 1.40

    C. None of the above

41. Andrea is watching TV and hears that the Dow Jones Industrial Average is hitting new highs. Andrea immediately goes to her platform and puts on a short binary contract. Which underlying market is she trading?

    A. DJIA NYSE

    B. Wall Street 30

    C. CBOT E-mini Dow Futures

42. A trader looking to be bullish on the U.S. dollar can watch which of the following instruments?

    A. DXY

    B. UUP

    C. UDN

43. An at-the-money binary option is at $55. It means that it will likely settle at $100 if it is less than two hours from expiration. Do you agree?

   A. Yes
   B. No

44. An in-the-money binary option strike price will always be trading at a price higher than an at-the-money strike price. Do you agree?

   A. Yes
   B. No

45. A trader has $2,500 cash in his account and decides to put on $2,500 worth of positions. He is allowed to do this.

   A. True
   B. False

46. Joe put on a short position on a binary contract when the bid was $75. The bid moves to $85 and the ask moves to $90, after unexpected news. Joe decides to close his position. What are his profits, if any?

   A. $75
   B. $100
   C. $15
   D. $25

47. Steven put on a long position on a weekly binary for a premium of $75 on Monday morning. Joe waited and purchased the same binary option for $75 cost on Wednesday morning. Joe told Steven he has less risk because he waited to confirm his trade. Do you agree?

   A. Yes
   B. No

48. The binary option contract on gold has as its underlying market which of the following:

   A. London spot fix gold
   B. Comex gold futures contract
   C. South African Krugerrand one-ounce price

49. The binary option contract on the Aussie dollar has as its underlying market which of the following:

    A. AUD/USD CME futures contract.
    B. The Australian exchange
    C. Reuters spot quotes
    D. Nadex report of spot prices

50. The Federal Reserve Board is scheduled to release a decision on interest rates at 2 P.M. Bob wants to put on a trade to play a big move. Which of the following binary contracts will react the least to the announcement?

    A. U.S. 500
    B. USD/CHF
    C. USD/JPY
    D. EUR/USD

51. The binary contract on the S&P 500 has as an underlying market which of the following:

    A. SPDR (Standard & Poor's depositary receipts)
    B. S&P 500 Cash Index
    C. CME E-mini S&P 500 futures contract
    D. CME S&P 500 futures contract

Find the Answers

Go to www.binarydimensions.com/answers to get the right answers to this test! For more tests and answers, go to www.binarydimensions.com/tests.

Appendix B: More Training Tools and Tests

The focus of this book's appendices is to allow you to test your knowledge of the concepts and strategies covered in this book and to know where to go for more information. Of course, the best form of knowledge is experiential. There is no substitute for putting on trades. However, with binary option trading tools and training, the evolution toward profitable trading is more probable.

Since binary option trading is new, at this time there are few tools that are available to the trader to help improve his or her trading. In response to the lack of trading tools, a binary option trading toolbox has been created. It includes a unique one-stop place for apps relating to binary option trading. These include:

Online fundamental and technical checklists: Traders will be able to access numerous detailed checklists that provide a step-by-step approach for evaluating over 20 different underlying markets. For every underlying market there are technical and fundamental analysis checklists and trading tips!

Binary trading education modules: These modules provide an evolutionary path from beginner to advanced stages of trading binary options. They include learning management systems that pace the trader through the modules and test their skills and knowledge.

Trade of the Week: Real trading examples of winning binary option trades by real traders. This allows learning by example.

Coaching: One-on-one coaching for traders looking for intense trading.

Education webinars: Webinars and special expert appearances by leading binary option traders.

Trade action alerts: Access to trading alerts for in-the-money; at-the-money; out-of-the-money opportunities.

Find out more about the binary option trading toolbox at www.binarydimensions .com.

Index